HANDBOOK ON MANAGEMENT THEORIES

Prince Jide Adetule

AuthorHouse™
1663 Liberty Drive
Bloomington, IN 47403
www.authorhouse.com
Phone: 1-800-839-8640

First published by AuthorHouse   06/09/2011

ISBN: 978-1-4389-4801-0 (sc)
ISBN: 978-1-4389-4800-3 (hc)
ISBN: 978-1-4634-0243-3 (e)

Printed in the United States of America

Acknowledgement

I am immensely grateful to a number of persons who have contributed in no small measure to the successful completion of this Handbook. I wish to mention Dr. J.U.J. Onwumere, Senior Manager, Strategic Management Division, United Bank for Africa Plc who took the arduous task of going through all the manuscripts and offered immeasurable inputs. Also my good friend, Mr. Jossy Nkwocha, General Editor, Newswatch Magazine and Dr. M. A. Aluko, former Head, Department of Business Administration and Co-coordinator MBA, University of Lagos, for painstakingly going through the manuscripts. My wife of inestimable platinum, Princess 'Bola Adetule, for her intellectual criticisms. I also wish to specifically mention Prof. Harold Koontz who coined "Management Theory Jungle", my intellectual debt is to him and other academicians and practitioners who have contributed significantly to the field of management and whose works have been quoted and used by me in writing this book such as; Profs. L. Gulick, Glueck and Leon C. Megginson et al from whose books I got some selected management authors' pictures and landmarks; courtesies of:- Roland G. Greenwood, Historical Pictures Services, Chicago, Western Electric Photographic Services, Baker Library, Harvard University, (Graduate School of Business Administration) and New Jersey Bell. I cannot forget Mr. Eben. B. Ojo (my mentor), Prof. (Chief) Nnamdi Asika, Prof. Aloy Ejiogu, Dr. Ben Oghojafor, Prof. J.A.T. Ojo, Dr. Faluyi, Dr. Ekpo and Mr. Samuel I. Akomolafe. Others are Mrs. Mairo Y. Bashir, General Manager, (General Admin., Property and Corporate Affairs) United Bank of Africa Plc., Mr. Ogie Eboigbe, Head, Corporate Affairs Division, United Bank for Africa Plc., Mrs. Bunmi Akinkugbe, Princess Ademurewa Kosoko, Margaret E. Nyamse, Ajan Agbor, Princess Bimbo Ademola-Bawallah, Mrs. Sylvia Etim, Mr. Ben. Ikwenobe, Wilson Okoh-Esene, Ms. Abeke Shoda, Mr. Isaiah Adeosun, Carol Chukwura (Finecarol), Femi Onasanya, Mr. E. Bazuaye, Mrs C. Okoro, Marshal C. Nwokorie, Bedford Okei, Joseph Adebayo, TOS Adeniran, Deji Ligali, Eustace Nosike, Mrs. Funke Adeniji, Timothy Ogunjimi, Chidi Uba, Wasiu Olalekan, Akpan Emmason, Christopher

Ikhelege, Mrs. Esther Obiakor, Mrs. Titi Bello, Cynthia Osobase and Dr. Fapohunda, my lecturer in Comparative Management at the University of Lagos, without his inquisitive and helpful class I could not possibly have developed and sustained an interest in management theories. Others who gave tremendous support to this Handbook include my sister and brothers: Princess Aduke Adetule-Oso, Prince Adetunji Adetule and Prince 'Tope Adetule. In addition, members of Erijiyan Socialight Klob (ESK), Staff of GOAM Print especially, Pastor Gabriel Ogunjemilusi, Messrs. James Olowo and Olagadeyo Kehinde, who did the layout of the first edition, I am also beholden to staff of United Bank for Africa Plc. and Centre for Management Development Libraries, my numerous friends, both in my office, across the African continent and indeed the whole world who are source of inspiration to me but time and space will not permit me to mention their names.
I thank them all.

Lastly, I accept the sole responsibility for any possible error of omission and commission especially the grouping of authors and would be extremely grateful to the readers if they bring such mistake to my notice.

Prince 'Jide Adetule,
badetule@yahoo.com
Erijiyan-Ekiti, Nigeria.

Dedication

To the Almighty **GOD** through His only begotten son **JESUS CHRIST** who has sent me to this terrestrial realm to achieve a purpose, to him be honour, the glory and adoration. Also to HRH Oba A. A. A. Adetule Royal Family, Late Omo-Oba John Alafiaji Adetule and my late mother, Olori Christianah Olayemi AdeTunrinle Adetule who invested very much in me but died too soon to enjoy the fruits of her labor. My better half, Olori Rachael Olubola Adetule and our children; Prince Richard Adedeji Adetule Jr., Princess Rachael Adeyemi Adetule and Prince John Adeola Adetule J II. Lastly, to all lovers of education, especially Late Chief Obafemi Awolowo "Oduduwa Jr." whose Free Education programme helped to educate mankind, including the writer.

Preface

When I was preparing for my final year examinations at the University of Lagos, I came about the phrase "Management Theory Jungle". I became fascinated and decided to find out why Prof. Koontz chose to coin this for my favorite course. I also noticed that students of Comparative Management did not seem to know the Schools to which contributors of Management Theories belong. I therefore decided to embark on the writing of this handbook by bringing out clearly the classification of the various Schools and their contributions to the study of Management. Each chapter is devoted to each School of Thought for easy reference and understanding. This is a deliberate attempt to enable students, researchers and practitioners see at a glance each School, the contributors and their contributions.

Prince 'Jide Adetule
Erijiyan-Ekiti

Foreword

Prince 'Jide Adetule's Handbook on Management Theories, is a well-researched, interesting and readable book. The painstakingly done catalogue of the Management Theories with the comprehensive list of management theorists and authors makes the book easily understandable. I am personally fascinated that in spite of office work-load, social problems in a society such as ours and home-front demands; someone still finds time to put this piece together as his contribution to enrich and widen mankind's intellectual horizon. It takes a resilient, determined and disciplined person to produce this kind of book. It is a testimony to Prince 'Jide Adetule as an organized person not only in his university days but also in his working life.

I sincerely hope that this effort will spur other working class people to write books, which will complement those already published by various eminent scholars both within and outside our universities. I therefore, wholeheartedly recommend this book for the use of all PhD, MBA, PGD and undergraduate students. Professionals and general readership will find this book an irresistible addition to their libraries.

Prof. Sola Fajana
Department of Industrial Relations and Personnel Management
Faculty of Business Administration,
University of Lagos
Lagos, Nigeria.

CONTENTS

CHAPTER ONE

INTRODUCTION OF MANAGEMENT

1.1 EVOLUTION OF MANAGEMENT

Management is as old as human existence, which started in the beautiful Garden of Eden. Adam was in charge to look after the garden. He could be regarded as the first Chief Executive Officer or Managing Director on earth. This was not all God gave him a helpmate to assist him. Eve became the first subordinate. Afterwards, the institution of boss and servant or super-ordinate and subordinate relationship was created. When the time came for Adam to take responsibility for his mistakes, he passed the buck to his sub-ordinate, he subsequently became the first person to be fired, retrenched or sacked. Looking back at the antiquity records and ideas relating to Management, one can go on and on through the days of Greek Philosophers, through the Middle Ages, through early civilizations of Sumer, through Babylon, Assyria, Egypt, Persia, Greece, China and Roman Empires. Also through Niccolo Machiavelli, the Catholic, the Cameralists of the sixteenth to eighteenth centuries, through the Feudal System (in the rural areas), the Guild Systems (in the urban areas), Cottage System of production and Factory System, this is the heartbeat of Industrial revolution.

However, modern history of Management Theory can be traced to the industrial revolution, which first took place on a grand scale in Europe in 1850. Before this time, which Prof. Gullick called "pre-scientific management period", what operated was the 'Craft Shop Era' for example the Blacksmith. During this period, land was the real thing. One needed to acquire status or rank and power before he could acquire land. There were two big institutions then: the Military and the Catholic Church, which acquired land. After 1850, there were capital, complex machines and products through industrial organizations. The problem therefore was how to manage and coordinate these resources. As a result of this, modern management commenced, i.e. Scientific Management 1880-1930. The Engineers taught the world "Industrial Management", which is largely production management. In the last half of the twentieth century, Management has developed considerably having many branches called "Theories"

1.2 MANAGEMENT DEFINED

Before any meaningful discussion can be held on Management, we need to know what the subject matter is all about. There is no known universally acceptable definition of Management. However, many definitions are commonly accepted. Some of them are:

a. Management is the art of getting things done through and with people.
b. Management is the process of planning, organizing, directing and controlling the effort of organization's members using all other organization resources to achieve stated organizational goals.

These are just two out of the lot. However, while definition (a) refers to Management as an **Art,** (b) sees it as a **Process.** The implication is that many authors, researchers, practitioners, etc have viewed management from various perspectives or ways. Since there is no single catholic definition acceptable to all, Management has been defined variously as an Art, Science, Function, Process, Profession, Resource and Concept. An understanding of the management concept can be viewed from several perspectives:-

i.   **Art:** This is high level of skills, proficiency, expertise and competence. Like Art, Management can be distinguished by its proficiency through studies, experiences, observations, skills, expertise and competence.
ii. **Science:** This is a body of knowledge acquired by method of science involving actions and results; Management is also a body of knowledge because it is studied for many years through theories.
iii. **Function:** This is a special duty or performance in the course of work or duty, that is, Planning, Controlling, Organizing and Directing. These are combined to make up Functions or Elements of Management.
iv. **Process:** This is a systematic way of doing things. All managers regardless of particular skills engage in or perform interrelated activities in order to achieve desired goals.

v. **Profession:** This is an occupation that requires intellectual proficiency that should meet four criteria.
    a. Make decisions based on certain general principles
    b. Attaining their status by meeting certain objectives, standard of performance and not by chance or favoritism; for example before one can become a professional Accountant, Banker, Public Relations Practitioner, he/she must pass CPA, ICAN/CIBN/NIPR examinations respectively.
    c. Having superior knowledge
    d. Guided by Code of Ethics.

vi. **Resource:** Management is what we use to get what we want. It is an indispensable resource that helps to effectively combine other resources (human and material) to achieve desired goals and objectives.

vii. **Concept:** Management is defined as a concept because of its universality; as Management is defined in Nigeria so it is defined the same way in Japan or the US. The only difference is its application, which is relatively "Culture bound".

1.3 MANAGEMENT THEORIES:

Management Theories originated from different principles at different times within the last fifty years. There are different Theories propounded by Management Practitioners and Theorists. These Theories are varied and emanated from different disciplines such as Science, Sociology, Anthropology, Psychology, and Mathematics and so on. The evolution of Management did not come into existence through consciously planned or structured patterns but rather as a result of revolutionary development in a historical sequence. It should be noted therefore that these Theories are uncoordinated, unrelated, scattered and in some cases, controversial. They generate a lot of confusion because they cut across all disciplines and because of this unpleasant scenario, Prof. Koontz called it "Management Theory Jungle" in 1961, the word "Jungle" connotes confusion. The erudite professor classified these theories into the Management Process/Traditional/Universal School, Empirical School, Human Behavior School, Social System School, Decision Theory School, and Mathematical School. However, there have been alignments and re-alignments in the classification of these Theories over the years. The old and new ideas of Management do not in any way conflict or replace each other rather they co-exist and complement one another especially the new Theories complementing the old ones.

In order to make these Theories more understandable and meaningful and get out of this confusion, efforts have been made to integrate or align the contributions of different people with conscious minds or those who are thinking the same way. They have been grouped as they are related with similar or common bearing or theme or thrust about a particular problem. It is therefore called **"SCHOOL OF THOUGHT"**. Each School has in its own way, made unique contributions to the study of management and the contributors are grouped under different Schools of Management as can be seen in the following chapters.

CHAPTER TWO

THE CLASSICAL OR UNIVERSAL SCHOOL

2.1 FEATURES OF CLASSICAL OR UNIVERSAL SCHOOL OF MANAGEMENT

- ☐ *Believes in one central authority.*
- ☐ *Believes that delegation of authority is very important.*
- ☐ *Believes that span of control should be well defined.*
- ☐ *Believes that there should be clear division between line and staff management.*

This School of Thought is further sub-divided into two groups or theories; the Classical Management or Organization and Scientific Management.

2.2 CLASSICAL MANAGEMENT THEORY

Classical is used to qualify things of great value, things that are traditionally accepted or long established. The forerunners in this School are Henri Fayol, Robert Owen, A. Small, J. D. Mooney, Charles Barbage and Max Webber. Under this Theory, there are two sub-approaches; Administrative and Bureaucratic

[A] ADMINISTRATIVE APPROACH:

This approach seeks ways of bringing rationality into the affairs of men and organizations. It focuses on increase production through the work of individual employee and also concerns with how the organization in totality should be managed so as to improve performance. The contributors are and their works are:

i.   **Henri Fayol** - A Frenchman and an industrialist. He is regarded as the father of Modern Operational Management Theory. He developed fourteen principles of management. He believed all businesses are the same world over, that is; businesses are universal. Little was known about him because his book was written in French language until it was translated into English in 1949. He identified common functions of management as Planning, Organizing, and Controlling. His contributions amongst others are codification of the Management principles such as:

a.   **Division of Labor/Work:** a manager should give an employee specialized job or activities to carry out. He said that specialization leads to efficiency and higher productivity

b.   **Authority and Responsibility:** staff or employee's responsibility should be commensurate with the authority given him or her.

c.   **Unity of Command:** an employee can only report to only ONE superior officer (no one should serve two masters).

d.   **Scalar Chain or Chain of Authority and Communication:** the formal line of authority or the chain of authority should be cleared and unbroken from top to bottom through the organogram/organizational chart in which information, directives, responsibility and obedience should flow.

e.   **Discipline:** ensures respect for rules and regulations and authority of command.

f.   **Unity of Direction:** one channel to direct related operations

g.   **Subordination:** one's interest is subordinated to the organization's interest

h.   **Remuneration:** adequate payment of wages and salaries

i.   **Centralization:** authority resides at the centre

j.   **Order:** people and the material should be found in the right place at the right time

k.   **Equity and Justice:** fairness to all

l.   **Stability:** the tenure of personnel must be stable, high degree of worker turn over should be discouraged

m.   **Initiative:** employee should be allowed to think, initiate ideas and execute plan of action independently

n.   ***Esprit de Corp*:** unity of effort through harmony of interest or teamwork

ii. **Luther Halsey Gulick III** was born on January 17, 1892 in Osaka and died on January 10, 1993 in New York. He was expert on public administration. His father was a physician and Camp Fire Girls founder. Gulick graduated from Oberlin College in 1914 and received his Ph.D. from the Columbia University in 1920. He agreed with Frederick Taylor that certain characteristics of organizations make an administrator to be effective. He was in accord with Max Weber in that organizations were hierarchical. He added the concept of span of control limiting the number of people a manager could supervise effectively. He also recommended unity of command because workers should know who they are responsible to in an organization. His homogeneity of work centered on the fact that an organization should not combine dissimilar activities in single agencies. This was the basis of Gulick's major contribution in the area of departmentalization. He expanded Fayol's elements of Management with popular acronym POSDCORB, which made him widely known. P=Planning; O=Organizing; S=Staffing; D=Directing; C=Coordinating; R=Reporting and B=Budgeting

Planning: Gulick said planning is working out in broad outline the things that need to be done and the methods for doing them to accomplish the purpose set for the enterprise. Planning is a futuristic idea of deciding in the present, what a company or person wants to do or achieve in future. Peter Drucker put planning as those who fail to plan, plan to fail; in the same manner, it is better to plan and fail, than not planning at all. Planning entails broad outline of what to be done and method to be used to achieve the goals. Planning does not work in isolation. To be able to plan effectively, one needs to know or determine the past activities, the present and future through forecast. Planning is very strategy in an organization. The objective of organization is an aim of what the organization intends to do and achieve them either in the short, medium or long run. It could be to capture or increase its market shares. The company needs to scan the opportunities available in the market, it either create a new market for its products, expansion of the existing market. It may also mean the introduction of new products. In order to achieve this, it must improve training facilities like changing from manual to full or partial computerization. Develop it workforce with modern marketing strategies. It must also prevent the organization from fallen into temptation or problems that might prevent development and implementation of programs. Planning also include adequate resources needed in an organization as a whole and departmental objectives such as human capital need, physical need, time, financial requirements, production capacity, distributions networks. Goals are therefore needed to achieve these specific targets that will be used to achieve various objectives. Planning is probably the most important aspect of human life and organization survival hinges on it. A company needs to follow some steps in planning in order to make head way. It should be aware of opportunities in environment, establishment of objectives, premises and assumptions, determination of alternative causes of action, which means planning is and must not be a one way jacket. If one's planning does not work well and give pre-determined results, you can pursuit the alternative action. Evaluate all alternative causes, select the best, and formulate a derivative plans. These are numerated by way of budgeting. The advantages of planning cannot be over-looked. It is an avenue to systematize thinking that is very healthy and useful to the top management echelon. Company's efforts are appreciated due to better coordination, company's objectives and policies are sharpened from time to time. Control and standardizations are products of performance development and guide against sudden shock. Performance and failure can be easily measured and predicted. The executives are fulfilled at the end, because of participatory and inputs of all organizational members because both Success and failure are shared. Adequate planning is an ante dose to failure.

Planning leads to better coordination, guide against sudden new developments that can cripple an organization who does not plan ahead, it off set the unexpected changes and uncertainty in the economic, it results in economical operations that would have been enormous if planning was not in place. It encourages systematic development and discourages fractures in the organizational quest for breakthrough.

Organizing making sure men and material resources are available and organized for the overall objectives of the enterprise. This entails division of labor, delegation of authority to individual, dividing the enterprise into different departments and units. It set out span of control and coordination of various units through line staff and technical heads

Staffing: the organization needs qualified personnel and therefore management functions includes recruitment or hiring, selects, retain and train lower cadre staff while middle and top staff are develop. Staffing sometimes refers to as hiring and used interchangeably. 'The whole personnel function of bringing in and training the staff and maintaining favorable conditions of work'

Directing: making sure everybody does his/her job efficiently and effectively. Directing involves motivation, communication, performance appraisal, discipline and conflict resolution amongst the workers. Gulick's opinion it that directing is a continuous task of making decisions and embodying them in specific and general orders and instructions and serving as the leader of the enterprise

Coordinating: the establishment of the formal structure of authority through which work subdivisions are arranged, defined, and co-ordinated for the defined objective and bring all activities and initiatives of various interrelating parts together in an organization

Reporting: workers under a supervisor's control should be kept within those to whom the executive is responsible and informed as to what is going on. It includes keeping himself and his subordinates informed through records, research, and inspection. It is suggested that six workers should be limited for effective supervision of a Manager

Budgeting: Management provides detailed forecast of revenue and expenditure of the organization. It constructs a model on how business will be run in relating to what goes with budgeting of planning, accounting and control both within and foreseeable future

iii.   Robert Owen - He was regarded as the father of Personnel Management and

Industrial Relations. He was one of the most successful industrialists in the early 19th century. He carried out an unprecedented experiment in the textile mills, which he managed in Scotland. Owen was an outstanding pioneer of management in his time, who was noted for his interactive with his workers.
- ☐   He visited his workers at home to find out how they lived and built housing Estates for them
- ☐   He founded a co-operative society for workers
- ☐   He reduced working hours
- ☐   Increased working age

- ☐ Introduced rating system.
- ☐ He provided meal for employees at factory.

iv. **Charles Babbage** - Invented mechanical calculator, which he called "Deferent Machine" He was a Cambridge professor of mathematics from 1828-39, he advocated the principle of Division of Labor and use of Time Study.

v. **Lyndall Fownes Urwick** - Lt. Col. Urwick was a British Army officer, and one of the greatest British management thinkers and writers of all times. He founded the Institute of Industrial Administration. He was a Management Consultant who authored ten-principles/articles on organization building namely:

1. **Objective:** that all organizations should have clearly defined objective for which they are set up.
2. **Specialization:** activities of members of an organization should be defined and confined to a single function.
3. **Co-ordination:** this is co-coordinating unity of efforts and harmonizing individual efforts.
4. **Authority:** there should be clearly defined lines of authority from the top to everyone in the organization.
5. **Responsibility:** super-ordinate should assume absolute responsibility for acts of his sub-ordinate.
6. **Principle of definition:** duties, authority and responsibilities should be written and communicated to all concerned.
7. **Principle of correspondence:** in every position, the responsibility and authority should correspond.
8. **Span of control:** He suggested for effective control, a manager should not supervise more than five or at most six direct sub-ordinates whose work "inter-lock", where no interlocking exists, the control could be more.
9. **Principle of Balance:** various units should be kept in balance.
10. **Principle of Continuity:** re-organization and re-engineering should be a continuous process.

vi. **William H. Newman** - He posited the Process of Learning. Learning is the psychology of acquiring knowledge, skills and its also involve change of attitude or behavior.

vii. **Richard Arkwright** - He contributed to continuous production, plant side planning, coordination of machines, materials, men, capital, factory discipline and division of labor, which mark him as a pioneer in the use of efficient management principles. Arkwright like Owen was equally interested in motivating workers for increased productivity. He maintained strict discipline among his workers and all considered him to be a fair man.

[B] BUREAUCRATIC APPROACH:

a. **Max Webber -** The great sociologist, who described the power of charisma as a certain quality of an individual personality, by virtue of which he is set apart from ordinary men and treated as endowed with supernatural, superhuman, or at least specifically exceptional powers or qualities. He developed the Concept of Typology of Bureaucracy. Webber, a German social historian, wrote a book titled. *The Theory of Social and Economic Organization.* His study of the development of Organization Theory and Capitalism is still the first and also provides the take-off point for sociological studies. He argues that a bureaucratic organization has five basic attributes namely:

1. **Division of Labor:** This involves specialization of tasks. Work should be broken down into components since nobody can perform all jobs, for example, someone in production, marketing, accounting, security, purchasing and quality control.

2. **Hierarchy of Authority**: This is arrangement of office from top to the lowest level of the organizational pyramid. It promotes co-ordination of activities and adherence to superior institution. All complex organizations today practice this feature.

3. **Rules and Regulations:** It states the right and responsibility of each position and individual. It promotes the use of fact and discourages individual judgmental

or discretional decisions. It makes employees actions uniform and stable.

4. **Impersonal Orientation**: Working environment is informal and formal, official decisions are made purely without sentiments or prejudice; all employees are fairly treated.

5. **Career Orientation:** Technical competence is the key to advancement in career path. Achievement and or seniority are the basis for promotion. Super-ordinate's assessment or evaluation of employee is based on employee's rare talents and must be defended against denial of promotion and arbitrary discharge to ensure continued loyalty to the organization.

b. **Stacy J. Adams** - Propounded the Equity Theory of Motivation. He said workers strive for justice and fair play in the place of work, for example:

☐ When employee gives time for work, he expects pay/ bonuses,

☐ When he gives skills, he expects job security.

c. **Sigmund Feud leo Festinger** - Developed the Dissonance Theory of Management.

He maintained that individual employees strive to maintain a balance between their cognitive belief and their behavior. Where there is inconsistency, psychological discomfort/dissonance is created.

d. **Emile Durkheim** – A French Scholar, who emphasized the idea that groups, through establishing their values and norms, control human conduct in any social organization.

2.3 SCIENTIFIC MANAGEMENT THEORY

(a) **Fredrick Winslow Taylor** - An American, who rose through the ranks – as apprentice, laborer, clerk, machinist, foreman, chief draftsman and lastly chief industrial engineer. He popularized the theory and is regarded as the father of the Scientific Management School and posited the concept of Management By Exception (MBE). His contributions under this school are:

i. Pioneering the development of science in management, which replaced the Rule of the Thumb Methods in management? He did away with guesswork.
ii. Scientific selection of workmen and the progressive teaching and development of workmen.
iii. Scientific education and development for selected workers.
iv. Paying workers on incentive basis i.e. tie salary to how much a worker can produce.
v. Let every worker be developed to his/her highest level or fullest capability.
vi. Institute friendly co-operation between management and staff.

He further states that:
- A large daily task: each man should have clearly defined task to accomplish daily.
- Standard condition: a worker is given standard condition and adequate tools to work with.
- High pay for a job well done, for example financial incentives.
- Loss of pay for failure.

(b) Harrington E. Emerson - He championed welfare standardization in an organization. He developed the principles of efficiency and method of cost control. He also defined the manner in which efficiency of resources can be accomplished and twelve principles of efficiency, which eliminate waste and create wealth. Organizations today imbibe his contributions namely:

1. Organizations should have clearly defined objectives and every staff should familiarize with these objectives.
2. Managers should seek good counseling for solution to problems.
3. There should be strict adhere to organizational ideals
4. Effectiveness of other principles is crucial and depends on strict discipline
5. Principle of fair deal was advocated, which is in essence required that managers should be sympathetic, imaginative and above all just

6. Record keeping in all organizational matters should be reliable, immediate, adequate and permanent
7. There should be effective production scheduling and control techniques
8. Standardization of work and proper placement of each worker on the job
9. Standardization of work conditions and the environment will reduce waste by conserving both effort and money
10. Standardization of operations wherever possible will greatly enhance efficiency
11. Written standard instructions should be continually updated
12. Efficiency should be accordingly rewarded

(c)   Frank Bunker Gilbert - Developed Body Motivation in conjunction with his wife, Lillian Moller Gilbreth who on the other hand, propounded the Human Fatigue & Factor in Work Theory. She was particularly interested in the selection, placement and Training of personnel. Among their contributions to the study of management is the Development of position plan of promotion, which is intended to serve employee's development plan namely:

1. Employee does his present job, prepares for the next higher step, and trains his/her successor.
2. Combine talents to produce breakthrough in motion study and job simplification. Identification of the basic motions and time required for each hand and arm movement.

Lillian was widely acclaimed as the 'First Lady of Management". She died in 1972 at the age of 93.

(d) Henry L. Gantt - Developed Building Task and Bonus System, that is, sequencing production activities. He also invented the Gantt chart. Gantt was Fred Taylor's contemporary and was the first to see human relations in industry as an important element. He believed that scientific management should entail the study of problems according to scientific method, more so as these tasks or incentives are to motivate. This is simpler and more applicable than Taylor's approach. He also believed that training of workers should be the sole responsibility of the management. This is widely practiced all over the world today. He was the forerunner of modern technique as Program Evaluation Review Technique (PERT).

(e)   Carl George. Barth – He was an erudite scholar who invented the Slide Rule, a mathematical instrument of two parts, which slides upon the other for rapid calculation. He was best known for developing graphic methods of depicting plans and making better managerial control.

(f)   Edward A. Filene - His primary interest was in employees' training and evaluation. He has concern for the human element in business. He used part of his fortune to form "Twentieth Century Fund for Research," which is still in existence.

(g)   Louis D. Brandies - He coined "Scientific Management" at a meeting of engineers in October 1910.

(h)   Henry R. Towne - He was the first early scientific manager in the USA. Towne was the president of the Yale and Towne manufacturing company for 48 years during which he introduced.

  i.   Payment of guaranteed wage for individual worker
  ii. Standard work should be given to each department and determine costs of production
  iii. Equal share of gain to increase efforts among the management and staff of a department. This will ensure rewarding of only productive department

(i)   Frederick Halsey - He has the same line of thinking with Towne's ideas, which he summarized as follows:
  i.   Individual worker should be paid proportionally with the amount of work done
  ii. He favors sharing of profit formula, under which increases in productivity are also shared between employer and employee
  iii. Payment of worker's day should be on the basis of number of hours spent on the job

(j)   **Boulton M. and James Watt** - They are one of the earliest people to practice scientific management in England in 1800.They made the following contributions to management:

1. They place emphasis on forecasting, production planning and information that are useful to determine demand and supply of steam engines.
2. Determination of speeds of each machine and how much output that could be expected.
3. The speeds of each machine were further broken down into series of minor operations so that each worker's job could be systematically analyzed.
4. A wage payment system based on price rate approach was adopted on standardized tasks and knows the standard of bonus to be given on excess production
5. Keen attention was paid on motivation e.g. wage increase, insurance scheme, building of housing estates etc. so as to maintain morale of workers
6. Detailed accounting procedure was developed and put in place in the company, which cater for raw material, costs, labor charges, finished goods, inventory recording and other accounting issues.

(k)   **William S. Jevons** - He was a leading British economist and best known for his writing on the "Utility Theory of Value". He made two important contributions to management thought thus:-

i.   That improvement in the tools use by workers for operational duties could assist in lessening the worker's fatigue that is the more sophisticated the worker's tools or instruments are, the more productive he/she would be.
ii. That higher productivity could be achieved if the worker is given enough time each day, week or month at the most to rest so as to recover from fatigue and start work with a fresh energy. This is probably the reason for annual leave today.

2.4 GENERAL CONTRIBUTIONS OF THE SCHOOL TO THE STUDY OF MANAGEMENT

[1]   **Classical Management Theory** believes in the principles that can be generally applied to describe: (a) functional activities and (b) what managers do in an organization.

(a)   Functional Activities

Henri Fayol, who is widely regarded as leader of the Classical School posited six functional activities in an organization no matter the size. They are:

1. Technical Activity: - Production of goods & services
2. Commercial Activity: - Buying and Selling, Commerce and Distribution
3. Financial Activity: - Dealing in acquiring funds and capital
4. Security Activity -Protection of workers and company's property
5. Accounting Activity - Keeping records, profit & loss and costing.
6. Managerial/Element of Management:
    i.   Planning: study of future and arrangement of plan of operation
    ii. Organizing: making available men and material resources to the enterprise
    iii. Commanding: making the employees do their jobs
    iv. Coordinating and Controlling: uniting enterprise activities in line with the predetermined rules and regulations i.e. organization's policies

(b)   What Managers do in an organization include:
1. Assume responsibility for the action of their subordinates
2. Balance competing goals, ensures immediate attention and strike a balance between various goals; those that require prompt attention and others that require postponing.
3. Mediate and ensure harmonious working relationships amongst people they work with.
4. Acts as a diplomat. He is the official representative of his

division/department and represents his organization outside; dealing with customers, government officials and the public on behalf of his organization.

5. Conceptual thinking. He must be able to think analytically in both concrete and abstract terms on problems and find solutions to them.

6. Serves as a communication centre by virtue of his position. He receives processes and disseminates information both within and outside the organization.

7. Takes difficult decisions, at times, the company may be faced with financial problems or may want to layoff some employees who may even be his friend.

8. Acts as a politician. He will need to use his art of persuasion, compromise and crafty means just like politicians to achieve certain organizational goals. He can achieve this by joining a network of mutual alliances/coalitions with other managers to gain support in certain critical decisions or proposals.

[2]   **The Scientific Management Theory**, which is also labeled as "Productivity Approach"

a. Believes and is concerned with the means of improving the productivity of each worker using scientific methods.

b. Reducing cost of operation and boosting the returns on investment.

c. Increasing prosperity of the workers through higher pay and wages that accompany higher productivity. F. W. Taylor, the leader of the School posited the following, which are still relevant in the study of Management.

1. One best way of doing a particular job
2. One best way of selecting the worker that best suits the job
3. One best way of educating and developing the worker
4. One best way of encouraging management/labor relationship

[3]   **Other contributions of the school:**
i.   Identifying fourteen principles of management.
ii. Tasks of management.
iii. Identifying management as a skill that can be taught.
iv. Hierarchy structure shows the flow of authority from top to lowest level.
v.   Rules and Regulations that govern the conduct of everybody in an organization, the conditions of service and industrial relations matters.
vi. The best way of doing things lead to continuous search for efficiency.

2.5 CRITICISMS:

a. Stresses more on the machine and pays little attention to human beings as if machine can operate itself.
b. Prof. Hugo Munsterberg claimed that what managers do are great, rather than giving vague objective of what managers do by Henri Fayol and his team, a manager concentrates on current, special and ad hoc issues.
c. These are dysfunctional fallout such as:

   ☐ Rise of boredom that ultimately leads to lower productivity as a result of over specialization.
   ☐ A despotic specialist can hold the public or an organization to ransom.
   ☐ Impersonality can result in low morale among staff.
   ☐ Impersonal relations may breed frustration and conflict among old adults.
   ☐ Hierarchy can lead to distortion and blockage of information along the scalar chain.
   ☐ Red-tapism, conservatism, rigidity, over-conformity, strict compliance of rules and regulations can hinder result oriented at limited time.
   ☐ The results at which promotions are based, favor achievers at the expense of less talented superiors.

CHAPTER THREE

THE BEHAVIOURAL OR HUMAN RELATIONS SCHOOL

3.1 FEATURES: The following are the features of the Behavioral or Human Relations

School of Management

- □ *Stresses the importance of human beings in an organization.*
- □ *Believes that there is a direct relationship between good human relations and productivity.*
- □ *Stresses the importance of good managerial style.*
- □ *Employee participation on matters affecting them.*
- □ *Good communication, managerial skills, and interpersonal relations.*
- □ *There is a direct link between good managers and stable industrial society.*

Human Relations/Behavioral is another School of Management that takes precedence after the Scientific Management and the period lasted from 1930-50. While Scientific Management regards "Machine Problem as Human Problem or the Sales Problem", which features prominently in Management literatures. Human Relations regards human beings as the most valuable resource in an organization. Behavioral Management or Human Relations Management philosophies are inter-woven in their approaches to management studies. Behavioral emphasizes the importance of individual, while Human Relations pays attention to the social condition as well as interpersonal relations of workers in an organization.

3.2 CONTRIBUTORS TO THE SCHOOL ARE:

a.   **George Elton Mayo** – An Australian and a student of industrial history. He death with the Social problems in an organization. An Harvard University Professor and acclaimed as the father of the Human Relations Group. In his famous Hawthorne Studies and Experiment at Western Electric Company, Chicago, USA, he concluded that informal groups did the magic of increasing productivity. Mayo described an organization as a social system of cliques, grapevines, informal status, rituals, and a mixture of logical, non-logical and illegal behavior. All these are capable of oiling the increase in organization's productivity drive.

b.   **John R. Adair** - Developed human needs in an organization as exemplify in the following:

  i.   The functional approach to management/leadership style as against situational approach, which he said changed leadership constantly so as to have the better man for the job at all times.
  ii. He said there was no need of leadership in a group.
  iii. He touched on effective training for a leader.
  iv. He said that task needs must be well analyzed, and will help in the attainment of corporate set objective.
  v.   He maintained that individual needs should be analyzed.
  vi. Individuals join groups because of the benefits derivable from the group.
  vii. He advocated maintenance need.

c.   **Abraham H. Maslow** - Developed man's basic needs, which he called Hierarchy of Needs. He was a behavioral Psychologist who developed and contributed in no small measures towards Motivation with the concept of basic needs of man, which he categorized into five hierarchies of needs namely:-

  1. Physiological: these are food, clothing, and shelter
  2. Security: Protection against danger, job security
  3. Social: Love, affection, association with others
  4. Esteem/Ego: status, reputation, and mutual respect.
  5. Self-Actualization: Similar to self-fulfillment of McGregor's Theory Y.

6. Aesthetic and Cognitive Need: Management experts have added 'Aesthetic Need', things of beauty and 'Cognitive Need' the need to know and understand. The two needs now occupy the top most position on the pyramid.

d. **Frederick Herzberg** - Is one of the best behavioral Scientists who developed the "Job Enrichment and Two Factor Theory" namely Motivator/Hygiene/Satisfiers and Maintenance/ Dissatisfiers. The concept of duality.
1. Motivator/Satisfiers are intrinsic to the job and it produces job satisfaction and self-actualization.
ii. Maintenance/Dissatisfiers are things that do not provide motivation but merely prevent dissatisfaction in an organization.

e. **Douglas M. McGregor** - He discovered the human side of enterprise and formulated Theory **X,** reflects of pessimistic view of workers and **Y,** which takes optimistic view of workers. These are two opposing views or assumptions that represent more of the philosophy of human relations school.

Theory X states that:
1. The average human being has an inherent dislike for job and will avoid it, if possible.
2. The average person lacks ambition, dislikes work and responsibility but prefers to be directed, coerced, controlled and threatened with punishment to get his/her adequate effort towards meeting organization's objective. However, he wants job security and economic rewards.
3. The average person is resistant to change.
4. The average person is self-centered and indifferent to corporate objectives.

Theory Y on the other hand, states that:

i. The average person is not by nature passive/resistant to the organization's need.

ii. That experience of physical and mental effort in the work place is natural as play or rest.

iii. The average person does not lack ambition, dislikes work, responsibility, directed, punishment, coerced, controlled and threatened rather he leans under rewarding conditions to seek and accept responsibilities.

This is contrast to number (2) in Theory X.

The average person learns under ideal situation. He seeks and accepts responsibilities. He wants to exercise autonomy and creativity. This is relevant to self-actualization of Maslow's Hierarchy of Needs.

f.   William Ouchi - He popularized Theory Z that emphasizes on Trust, Subtle and Intimacy. This is middle level/ground between Theory X and Y. The theory integrates common business practices in the US and Japan into one middle frame work e.g. long term employment, Holistic Concern, etc.

g.   David C. McClelland - Described Achievement, Power and Affiliation needs of an individual as follows.

1. **Achievement:** This is motivation, which centers on the relationship between parental values and children's proclivity to future achievement; children and economic development. The basic dominant motive is achievement for example, the creative people such as Sales Men, Artists, and Scientists. The achievers think all the time, they like to take responsibility, solve difficult problems, set task with calculated risk. Achievers don't like to fail. They go with opportunity.

2. **Power:** The inner experience, the best position for achievement motivates a person in the corporate setting. People seek power, which can be Dominance, Manipulative, Social and Personal.

3. **Affiliation:** These people have reflect desire to interact with others. They hate to see their names in the black book – "Nice guy make bad boss". He concluded that:

i. The Executive group has the highest need for power and lower affiliation.

ii. The non-Executive group has the highest need for achievement.

h.   Chris Argyris - Developed the Psychology of the Individual in organization. His Theory centers on matured individual and those rigid organizational rules that hinder workers from fully utilizing their potentials. He said that:

a. The individual must value him/her self.

b. An opportunity in the place of work by making job more challenging, rewarding and giving more responsibility to the worker. In effect, effective leader moves subordinate from state of immaturity to maturity, state of dependence to independence.

i.   Rennis Likert - Postulated the Human Organization. Likert advocates "Ideal Organization" and lays emphasis on the morale of workers and need to interact with group. In his work on leadership, he deals with Systems 1- 4 on leadership style.

System 1 Authoritative- Exploitative
System 2 Authoritative-Benevolent
System 3 Consultative
System 4 Participative

He said that system 4, that is, Participative, is the most appropriate or ideal. In humanistic term, it ensures satisfaction for employee and maximum output and profit in organization. System 4 is likened to Theory Y while System 1 is likened to Theory X of McGregor's
Theory X &Y.

j.   Fritz J. Roethlisberger - Developed the social problem of organization.

k.   William Dickson - Contributed to the Social problem of organization

l.   **Robert L. Katz** - Is noted for his Skill classifications. Skill means ability that can be developed. He said skill is not in-born rather, it is related to performance. He provided three types of skills as:

a.   **Conceptual Skill:** Katz said this is very important to top management who see
the organization as a whole to the entire business world. They think analytically and 'foresee' the future to formulate policies and make complex decisions. They are proactive managers.

b   **Human Relations Skill:** Is ability to lead other workers, motivate them, and manage conflict amongst them. Managers must create a conducive-working environment free of rancor and acrimony. Middle management needs this skill more than other management levels though it is also applicable to all categories of management, but the degree of relevance diminishes from top to bottom.

c.   **Technical Skill:** This is ability to perform specific activities in the fields. Those in the technical aspect in organization, for example those in Engineering department needs this skill. It is relevant to lower line managers who must be knowledgeable and efficient in methods, procedures, and techniques. It also requires on the job training.

m.   **Peter Drucker** - In 1950, he introduced management techniques called Management By Objective (MBO) or Supervision By Result (SBR). This is a Participative management where subordinate and manager formulate objectives. He defined Effectiveness and Efficiency of managers as:

    a.   Effectiveness: Do things right
    b.   Efficiency: Do right thing at minimum cost.

n.   **Victor H. Vroom** – He postulated the noted for Expectancy Theory, which is [Motivation = Valence X Expectancy] and popularly called Valence Force.

o.   **Kurt Lewin** - Developed the Force Field Theory and posited that to increase productivity, we need to reduce noise in working environment. If there are disturbances in worker's environment, he cannot achieve productivity or achieve little productivity. The person doing the work and environment and forces, that is Human Behavior is a function of Person and Environment [HB= f(PE)].

p.   **Robert J. House** - He posited human behavior in organization and the Path-goal Theory of Leadership.

q.   **Alan C. Fillery** - Posited Human Behavior in organization.

r.   **D. Silverman** - Itemized the elements of Hawthorne experiment into six compartments as follows:

- That individual has "personality needs" and/or "generalized motives" which can be hierarchically arranged from physiological and safety and move to self-actualization need.
- The need and motives exerts direct influence upon behavior.
- Behavior can analyze the need and motive which are the bases.
- There is conflict between individual goal and that of organization, which must be resolved.
- The only way to resolve it is to change the organizational structure.
- The best form of organization is to harmonize workers' active participation in decision-making, less rigid and effective communication.

s.   **Clayton P. Alderfer** – He developed the Existence, Relatedness and Growth (ERG) Theory of Motivation, which is a compressed or merger of Abraham Maslow's five Hierarchy of Needs.

t.   **Abraham Zaleznik** – Understanding human behavior in an organization.

u.   **Dale S. Beach**– Management of people at work.

v.   **Robert R. Blake & Jane S. Mouton** - They developed Managerial Grid, which demonstrates leadership styles into two behavioral dimensions namely:
   a. Leader whose concern is for production.
   b. Leader whose concern is for people.

w.   **Edward E. Lawler III** – Described the casual correlation of the Need Hierarchy concept.

x.   **Edgar H. Schein**– Posited understanding human behavior in an organization

y.   **Warren Bennis** - Understanding human behavior in an organization

z.   **Mary Parker Follett** – an American philosopher and a consultant on matters relating to selecting and maintaining co-operation amongst people in business. She first adapted social science to industry and developed new concept of management and relations with industrial groups. She paid less attention to the individual in an organization while she concentrated on groups in industry.

aa.   **Vilfredo Pareto** - A French-Italian who is regarded as the Father of Social System Approach to Organization and Management. He viewed society as an intricate cluster of interdependent units or elements and that system consists of many sub-systems.

bb.   **Walter Dill Scott** – He wrote on Application of Psychological Concepts to Advertising and Marketing as well as Personal Management Practices of Effective Selection.

cc.   **Harold Koontz** - He coined the Jungle of Management Theories. The confusion in different authors from various disciplines of human endeavor propounding theories in management

dd.   **Leonard R. Sayles** – Develop Human Behavior in an organization.

ee.   **Keith Davis** – He explained Human Behavior at work: Human Relations and Organizational Behavior.

ff.   **Peter J. Lawrence** – He observed that workers get or tend to be promoted to a level of their incompetency in an organization where hierarchy is practiced dogmatically.

gg.   **Thomas Peters** – Identified characteristics of companies

hh.   **Robert Waterman** – He also identified characteristics of companies.

ii.   **Seebohm B. Routree** – He developed and applied various personnel techniques

jj.   **Robert Tannenbaum** – He posited a Behavioral Science Approach to Leadership and Organization.

kk.   **Phillips Selznick** – He used knowledge of sociology in management.

ll.   **Robert Dubin**– Used Human Relations in administration.

mm.   **Harold J. Leavitt** – He developed managerial psychology on individual, peers and group in an organization.

nn.   **Hugo Munsterberg** - A Harvard University professor, a German Psychologist and the father of industrial psychology and industrial efficiency. In his book, *"Psychology and Industrial Efficiency"* he highlights the objective of industrial psychology and noted the following, which are necessary in an organization.

  i.   How to find people whose mental qualities best fit for the work they are to do.
  ii. Understand psychological condition as the greatest and most satisfactory output that can be obtained from the work of every worker.
  iii. How workers can influence business in order to achieve the best possible result for example providing staff canteen, staff bus, staff housing scheme/estate and so on.
  iv. Mutual interest between management and labor.

He concluded that managerial work is blended with three roles, which are the behavioral pattern expected of an individual/manager within a social unit of business enterprise. The roles are inherent in function and they focus on:

  1. **Interpersonal/Contact Role:**
- **Leader:** The manager is responsible for staffing, training, activation and motivation of his subordinates**.**
- **Figure Head:** The manager is a symbolic head of his department and performs ceremonial jobs for example welcoming visitors, attending

subordinate's wedding ceremony, taking customers out for lunch, and so on.

- **Liaison:** He maintains a network of outside contacts with the organization's various publics.

2. Informational Role:

- **Monitor:** He is the nerve centre of internal and external information. He monitors unfolding events in the environment by seeking and receiving varieties of information.

- **Disseminator**: He transmits information received from inside and outside the organization, which might be of tremendous benefits to influence decision-making in the organization.

- **Spokesman:** He transmits information to the organization, outsiders or general public about the organization's plans, policies, actions, results and represents the company in public ceremonies. Example of this manager is the Public Relations Executive (PRE).

3. Decisional Role:

- **Entrepreneur**: Manager scans the organization and the environment for opportunities. He designs, initiates jobs and brings new technology to the job performance.

- **Disturbance Handler:** When the organization faces crisis, the manager finds quick solution, for example, when his organization requires stock at short notice, he quickly looks for suppliers or when there is labor unrest he finds solutions to the problem.

- **Resources Allocator:** He allocates both human and material resources optimally. He also schedules his time and prepares financial budget.

- **Negotiator:** He negotiates and hires new employee(s), and provides conditions of work and compensation to such employees. He represents the organization in major negotiations for example contract with government, suppliers and interacts with consulting firms.

oo.   **Oliver Sheldon –** He said that a manager must determine a proportion balance between things of production and humanity of production.

pp.   **Mc Farland-** He defined leadership as ability of an individual to influence other to work beyond their ordinary levels to achieve goals.

qq. **Davis & Newton-** They also defined leadership as a process of helping others to work enthusiastically towards objective. They said Leadership is a function of Leadership himself or herself, the People being led, Task or purpose to be accomplished and Situation/environment in which leadership is taken place. Leadership is therefore the combination of all that can be expressed in this equation as L=f(L,P,T,S).

rr. **Henry A. Murray:** He provided the exploration in personality i.e. the study of personality.

3.3 GENERAL CONTRIBUTIONS OF THE SCHOOL TO THE STUDY OF MANAGEMENT

1. The School is concerned with the way of increasing productivity through boosting of the workers' morale.
2. The School shows how human beings bring aspect of personality and behavior to work
3. It identifies the source or types of motivation.
4. It explains the leadership nature in an organization.

3.4 CRITICISMS:

a. The School over-stretched the role of leadership and supervision.
b. It neglects formal and technological structures in an organization.
c. There is an unclear correlation between good human relations and productivity, because of super-impose tendency of manager in getting things done by employing both stick and carrot to survive.

CHAPTER FOUR

THE MANAGEMENT SCIENCE OR QUANTITATIVE SCHOOL

4.1 FEATURES OF THE MANAGEMENT SCIENCE OR QUANTITATIVE SCHOOL ARE

- ☐ *Makes use of statistics and mathematics*
- ☐ *Applies science methodology*

This School belongs to the integrative approach and is a modern version of Scientific Management, which is variously called Quantitative Approach, Quantitative Analysis, Operations Research, Decision Science, System Analysis, System Science and Analysis for Decision Making. The authors of this School are group of mathematicians, physicists and scientists. They started in Great Britain at the beginning of World War II to solve complex problems in warfare through the quantitative tools, which are the hallmark of the Management Science School. They use scientific methodology in solving complex management problems. They also employ mathematical techniques for modeling and use them to solve decisional/managerial problems in areas of planning, controlling and decision making. This is called Operations Research (OR) and Analysis. They emphasize that the bulk of Management activities are to make decisions; as such, a number of models were designed to assist management. These are:

- ☐ Decision theory
- ☐ Break Even Analysis
- ☐ Inventory allocation
- ☐ Waiting line
- ☐ Simulation
- ☐ Capital budgeting
- ☐ Cash flow
- ☐ Production scheduling
- ☐ Network
- ☐ Planning manpower programme
- ☐ Computer technology

4.2 CONTRIBUTORS TO THE SCHOOL:

a.   **Eli Whitney** - He is one of the pioneers in this School. He invented cotton gin and developed a mathematical model of reducing manufacturing cost and efficient use of cotton gin.

b.   **Mathematicians**

c.   **Physicists**

d.   **Scientists**

4.3 GENERAL CONTRIBUTIONS OF THE SCHOOL TO THE STUDY OF MANAGEMENT

1. The extensive use of scientific methodology (statistics and mathematics) to solving complex problems in an organization.
2. The Operations Research (OR) has considerably increased management's capacity to cope with the ever-increasing complexity and environmental influence.
3. The use of computer memory in aiding decisions and solving management problems.

4.4 CRITICISMS:

However beautiful the above contributions are, it has been largely criticized that:

1. There are many behavioral or human relations' problems, which cannot be solved with mathematical tools.
2. Also mathematical problems cannot be solved using the human approach.

CHAPTER FIVE

THE SYSTEM SCHOOL

5.1 FEATURES OF THE SYSTEM SCHOOL OF MANAGEMENT ARE:

- ☐ *Emphasizes effective planning, control and decision-making.*
- ☐ *Sees organization as a whole*
- ☐ *All parts work together for organizational goals and objectives.*

According to Professor Harold Koontz, a system requires physical, human and capital resources to be interrelated and co-ordinated within internal and external environments of an organization. System Approach emphasizes that a system consists of interrelated parts or components or sub-systems such as people, structure, tasks and technology, which have an identifiable boundary or frontiers from the environmental super-system. Any activities in a section of the system will affect the whole system. It believes that problems are best solved by looking analytically at the organizational problems as a system and its inter-relatedness and inter-dependency of all parts to the whole system. There is need therefore for all parts in the organization to work harmoniously and relate synergistically; that is the whole is greater than the parts.

5.2 CONTRIBUTORS TO THE SCHOOL:

Chester Irving Barnard - Provided systematic analysis of administrative behavior within the framework of social sciences. He popularized the concept of effectiveness, which he relates to achievement of organizational objectives and efficiency that deals with satisfaction of employees' needs.

b.   **Herber A. Simeon** - Extends Bernard's view to organization and behavior using Behavioral Sciences. He sees organization as inducement exchange for work. An employee will remain in an enterprise if he believed that the inducements are larger than his input. Also he believes that administration in an organization is a rational decision making process capable of influencing human behavior.

c.   **D. Katz and R.L. Kahn** - They developed system model that represent an organization as an open system:

- [ ] **Input-Throughput-Output:** A business organization utilizes resources (human and materials) from environment in one form or the other. It converts or transforms into finished products or services and exports same back to the environment for consumption.
- [ ] **Equilibrium**: Input-output is cyclical in nature. The circle of production input-output is continually maintained between series of events to maintain equilibrium.
- [ ] **Negative Entropy:** This is a natural process of decay, death and dis-organization. Negative entropy is the process by which decay is arrested/ prevented through importation of more energy than it gives to the system for example cash, moral, resources, which are used as strength. All open system fights against liquidation of company due to embezzlement, hence a periodic auditing to guide against this.
- [ ] **Differentiation:** Individual parts perform their duties with greater elaboration and specialization. There are standard operating procedures, formal delegation of authority and responsibilities. Open system creates opportunity of sub-systems; hence an organization operates more branches.
- [ ] **Equifinality:** This is an organizational design to reach its level of final states from different initial conditions. Some organizations may choose acquisition; some may build a new plant. Also all the sub-systems work towards achieving the overall goals of an organization.
- [ ] **Steady State and Dynamic Homeostasis**: imported energy is used to offset entropy characterized by a steady state by adjusting to the situation. Government adjustment of policies to the wishes of the people is an example of dynamic

homeostasis, so also an organization must prepare for changes in the dynamic environment it is domiciled.

☐ **Feedback**: This is necessary to rectify any deviation and evaluation of set objective to see whether it is on course. Negative feedback serves as good device of correcting variation in performance and thus serves the purpose of a thermostat.

d. **E.F. Huse** - He defined system as a series of interrelated or interdependent parts, such that the interaction of any of the parts affects the whole. In system, thinking should replace linear thinking.

e. **Ludwing Von Bertalanffy** - A biologist, he viewed science from the perspective that each discipline composed of interrelated set of elements functioning as a whole. The human body is perhaps the best known example of a system. He said the survival or failure of the system dependent on the interrelation of the sub-systems and their contributions to the overall purpose of the system.

5.3 GENERAL CONTRIBUTIONS OF THE SCHOOL TO THE STUDY OF MANAGEMENT

1. The School lays emphasis on effective planning, controlling, and decision-making.
2. It views as secondary the idea of efficiency, while planning takes the first step.
3. Ability to cope with increased complexity and also environmental influence.
4. System perspective enables managers to easily maintain a balance among the needs of various parts of the organization.
5. The importance of feedback in quality control is an evidence of System School's contribution to the study of management.

5.4 CRITICISMS:

a.   A breakdown of a part should not have constituted a breakdown of the whole organization.

b.   Nobody should be seen as a stumbling block to the overall objective of the organization.

c.   Absence of a part should not mean a dead knell for the others, for example, a department that is cost centre can be discarded instead of draining the organization all in the name of interdependency/ interrelationship.

CHAPTER SIX

THE CONTINGENCY/SITUATIONAL OR ALL DEPENDS SCHOOL

6.1 FEATURES OF THIS SCHOOL ARE:

- *The kind of environment in which the company operates will dictate the kind of*
- *managerial style.*
- *Mechanistic approach is strong on efficiency and is appropriate in an unchanging*
- *environment.*
- *Everybody obeys and plays it by the rules.*
- *Organic approach is appropriate where innovation and creativity is welcomed.*
- *There is no rigid system of procedures; workers can play it by the rules.*
- *Job function of both staff and line managers may change/ rotate every day.*

This School also belongs to the Integrative Approach. The diagram below shows different approaches of the school:

6.2 ALL SCHOOLS OF MANAGEMENT:

The researchers and consultants who harnessed the concepts of all Schools of Management, that is, the Universal/Classical School, Behavioral/Human Relations School, Management Science/Quantitative School and System School, came up with Contingency/Situational/All Depends School in the 70s. Situational/Contingency School lays emphasis on the fact that no single design is the best for all problems or situations. Hence, solution to problems is a function or depends on factors particular to different situations of the environment. Furthermore, problems are contingent upon factors unique to different situations. It is therefore called "All Depends Theory".

6.3 MECHANISTIC APPROACH:

a. **Tom Burns** - He propounded Mechanistic Model under Contingency Approach. He used a close system of Management similar to Classical Approach, that is:

1.   Lines of authority are clear
2.   Everyone adheres to chain of command
3.   Distinction between line and staff authority/managers
4.   Most important decisions are delegated

However, this system is seen to be

- □   Bureaucratic
- □   Leadership is directive
- □   Authoritarian
- □   Span of control is narrow

6.4 ORGANIC APPROACH:

b. **G.M. Stalker** - Developed organic type of Contingency Approach. This is similar to Behavioral or Humanistic Approach where:

1.   Jobs are changing.
2.   Lines of authority not so clear.
3.   Opportunity to speak to boss directly.
4.   Jobs of staff and line managers are rotated i.e. job enlargement.
5.   Decision is decentralized; therefore, subordinate can make decisions.
6.   Jobs are moved, supervision is more general and the span of control is wider than mechanistic.

6.5 CONTRIBUTORS TO THE SCHOOL:

a.   **Burns** and
b.   **Stalker** are British researchers that sought to know the best organizational structure that is best for different types of industries. Apart from Burns and Stalker, the following authors also contributed tremendously to the School.
c.   **Joan Woodward** – A British woman, who focused her attention on technological factor, of Organization Structure or Building. She wanted

to know why organization's structure has no relationship to success. Her studies include:

    i.   Small units batch production companies producing one at a time specialized and prototype unit job for customer.

    ii.   Mass/Large batch production that is mass production.

    iii.   Long-run continuous process production for example chemical or oil companies. Her conclusions on the above are that in i & ii

- ☐ Management emphasizes less definition of duties.
- ☐ Greater delegation of authority.
- ☐ More permissive management.
- ☐ Loosely organized work groups.
- ☐ Less focus on organizational problems.

    iv.   Management tends to use line staff in organization closed supervision.

- ☐ Elaborate control techniques
- ☐ More written communication.

Her conclusion stems from the fact that optimum organizational structure depends upon the different industrial technological process. She shows that Organizational Structure and Human Relations are function of existing Technology/technological Situation [OS + HR=f (TS)]. She said that mechanistic type of organization is best fixed for mass production technology while; the organic is best for a unit craft or continuous process technology such as gas refinery.

d.   **F. E. Fielder.** - Theorized the leadership/membership relationship, which is contingent upon position and power, test structure and leadership/members relationship.

e.   **Lawrence and Lorsch** – Both posited that the degree of differentiation and integration depends on variability of the environmental forces.

f.   **Rosemary Stewart** - Found out that similar jobs may be done or undertaken differently by different managers not only in terms of tasks they initiate, emphasize or neglect. She argued that managerial effectiveness is contingent upon choice management demand and constraints implicit in the job.

g. **Joseph L. Massie** - Identified four cardinal factors that are very important to aManger
  i. The nature of the people in the organization
  ii The type of task and technology
  iii The environment within which an organization operates
  iv The degree of change and uncertainty the organization faces

6.6 GENERAL CONTRIBUTIONS OF THE SCHOOL TO THE STUDY OF MANAGEMENT

1. The School's contribution arose from the shortcomings of the other Schools of Management and they have taken care of these shortcomings.
2. The Approach is an amalgamation or product of other Schools of Management, hence they are called the "Situationalists".
3. It recommends total rejection of 'one best way of organizing, under all situations' and emphasizes consideration of organizing members and the external pressures facing them in reaching decision.
4. Fitting organizational structure to various contingencies by extending contingency to job design, leadership, group dynamics and power relationship.

6.7 CRITICISMS

1. The School was sharply criticized in that if everything depends on another it then means there is **No Reality.**
2. It looks for weaknesses in other Schools of Management Thought without developing its own principles that can be followed.

CHAPTER SEVEN

THE TOTAL QUALITY MANAGEMENT

7.1 INTRODUCTION

Total Quality Management (TQM) can be referred to as the "Sixth" School of Management in the sequential evolution of Management Theories. The emergence of Total Quality Management began as an American management philosophy in the 1920s died in America, took root in Japan and ultimately returned to flourish in the US and other Western nations. Dr. Edward W. Deming is regarded as the father of TQM with Dr. M. Juran, are two Americans that exported Quality Concept to Japan and called it Quality Circle. Kaoru Ishikawa, a Japanese expert played a major role in this by giving the world the Ishikawa Diagram. The Japanese recognized the fact that management fundamentals/principles/concepts/techniques are universal, only the applicability, practicability and transferability are contentious issues that are hotly debated amongst management experts. The Japanese blended TQM concept into their culture and made it work like magic. The culture of the people is the only thing that differs from one country to another. It is a matter of recognizing the peoples' diverse cultures. The whole world today is witnessing the industrial giant in Japan, that small island with little or no resources. TQM which is an acronym for Total Quality Management were explained by Joseph and Susan Berk (1951) as follows:

Total: That everyone in the organization is involved in the final product/service to the customer.

Quality: Is not just luxury, goods/services are described in a way that leaves no room for subjective opinion. Quality therefore means conformance to requirement that allows the measurement of quality. When speaking the same language of quality, everyone should understand it.

Management: TQM is a managing process; it does not just happen by accident. It means effective management of all available resources of people, system, tool and technique. TQM is therefore a change agent aimed at producing a customer-driven organization. TQM has four very unique philosophies namely:

a. Customer focus
b. Continuous improvement
c. Defect prevention or zero defects
d. Quality recognition is shared by all, that is, universal responsibility

Total Quality Management can be defined as combination of the people and system working harmoniously together for the ultimate benefit of the customer. It is also an excellent attainment of organizational goal. It is a structure and system for meeting and exceeding customer's expectation. TQM that engulfed the entire globe in the early eighties is a call to organizational excellence and could be said to be a customer-oriented concept, which is aimed at enhancing quality performance, through effective combination of features of previously propounded management tools such as:

Management by Objective (MBO)
Strategic Management (SM)
Organization and Method (O&M)
Work Study (WS)
Target Management (TM)
They form a unique tie in quality product/service, cost reduction, increased productivity, effective customer delivery system and greater efficiency.

7.2 THE MAJOR CONCEPTS OF TQM ARE TO:

☐   achieve quality in everything
☐   Do the right thing right first
☐   strive for customer's satisfaction
☐   Team building should be the watchword
☐   Practice proactive management

- ☐ Motivate employees
- ☐ Reduce waste
- ☐ Practice TQM

TQM as a management function aims at achieving organizational objective by creating a sustained quality product/service for its customers. According to Lee Iacocca when he advertised for Chrysler, that the company has three rules: "Satisfy the Customer, Satisfy the Customer and Satisfy the Customer. The way to achieve this is effective:

- ◊ Use two-way communication strategy
- ◊ Create discussion group to brainstorm on issues
- ◊ Build a link between the organization and its publics
- ◊ Work with colleagues (Seniors/Peers/Juniors) well.
- ◊ Woo more customers and service the existing ones
- ◊ Reduce over-head
- ◊ Improve performance
- ◊ Cost effectiveness
- ◊ Ensure few delay
- ◊ Remove mistake
- ◊ Emphasis on team management/building
- ◊ Focus on global standardization/internalization for instance (ISO 2000)
- ◊ Use TQM to market organization's products/services by tangiblising intangibility
- ◊ Sound conceptual and pro-active thinking
- ◊ Business Process Re-engineering- an improved TQM aimed at achieving quality into perfection radically

It is pertinent to note that TQM has succeeded in changing the position of organizational pyramid by inverting it and placing the customer on the uppermost pedestal of the pyramid, that is Customer occupies the pinnacle of the pyramid, next in line is the workforce and then the middle management or various managers follows and finally the top management staff being supportive of the whole pyramidal frame so as to provide quality goods and services.

7.3 CONTRIBUTORS TO TQM CONCEPT ARE:

1. Walter A. Shewhart
2. Edward W. Deming
3. Joseph M. Juran
4. Douglas MacArthur
5. Kaoru Ishikawa
6. Taguchi Genichi
7. Phillip B. Crosby
8. 8. Feigenbaum V. Armand

7.4 GENERAL CONTRIBUTIONS OF TQM TO THE STUDY OF MANAGEMENT

1. Complete and unequivocal satisfaction of the customers shows that organization has regard and uncompromised commitment to the customers' expectation.
2. Re-defining the position of customer in inverted organizational model by placing customer on the uppermost position
3. It makes everyone in an organization to be customer focus and actively involved in final delivery of quality product/service to the customer
4. It enables the organization to embrace total commitment and satisfaction of Customer
5. Reduction of defect to zero
6. Continues improvement of product/service

7.5 BARRIERS OF TOTAL QUALITY MANAGEMENT

- ☐ Inertia and the power of tradition are not easy obstacles to overcome
- ☐ Lack of management commitment
- ☐ Lack of vision and planning
- ☐ Satisfaction with the quick fix and people are not easily involve

☐ Tool bound prevents process of change
☐ Quality management becomes bureaucratic
☐ Management does not change behavior

7.6 CONCLUSION:

Any organization that wishes to be counted amongst the stars in the firmament of the triple Á organizations, that is, first class companies in the new millennium must start imbibing TQM culture. All Schools of Management look at the management of an organization in totality from different perspectives. Each of the concepts is useful for particular setting. The problem a manager faces is deciding which of them is suitable to use in a certain situation. It should be noted that none of the Theories provides a broad base diagnoses for organizational problems. The search for the 'Best' Management Theory definitely continues.

CHAPTER EIGHT

THE BUSINESS SYSTEM

8.1 WHAT IS BUSINESS?

Business is a concept that cannot be easily defined and therefore has no universally acceptable definition, except for some working definitions acceptable over time. Business has been defined as the combination or summation of all activities concerned with the production and distribution of goods and services for consumption and making profit as compensation for the efforts. Although some businesses are not established for profit making and do not fall into the category of this definition, yet they are business organizations. Business can also be a social melting point or institution through which people organized for economic efforts in areas of production, marketing, financing and other related activities aimed at providing goods and services. It is the complexity of commerce and industry of the basic industry through processing, manufacturing and the network or auxiliary services such as distribution, banking, insurance, high purchase, law, management consultancy, transportation and so on. Business is therefore sum total of all activities to plan and organize the functions of satisfying the entire human race with primary aim of making profit through calculated risk and within the given legal and social framework in any given society.

8.2 BUSINESS SYSTEM:

What has distinguished human being from other creatures is the instinct value, ability to organize and engage in sophisticated development. Unlike others creatures, human being is able to satisfy their material needs through distribution of goods and services since creation. Perhaps, the only simple function of the people around the world is the attempt to satisfy their needs and want in an orderly manner. In modern society, the channel of achieving this is narrowing down by the day through various scientific discoveries, internet shopping and others at the convenience of one's room or office without meeting, knowing or having physical contacts with the sellers and buyers who are thousands of miles away. There are various networks of organizations and institutions to achieve this. This is commonly refers to as Business System. Wherever goods and services are been produced and marketed is qualified to be called Business System. Business System or Economic System is one of the three disciplines that jointly rule the world. Others are Management or Politics and the Law or Judiciary, which I acronym as PEL - Politics, Economics and Law. Business is regarded as the back bone as well as bed rock of any society. There are evidences that points to the direction of prosperity and growth of country that measured and develop its Business activities. The industrialized nations are highly sophisticated with mass production and the consumers dependent directly on the availability of goods and services that are distributed by its business system at twenty-four-seven. In contrast, under-developed nations are still relatively depending to a large extend, on mass market production volume in-flow from the advanced countries for their domestic needs. Any country wishes to grow must take proper attention into its economic activities; otherwise it will perpetually remains beggar to prosperous nations.

CHAPTER NINE

THE BUSINESS CONCEPTS

9.1 BUSINESS ENVIRONMENT

The environment within which an organization domiciles or operates is divided into Internal Environment and constitutes men, machine, material and place. They all interact within the work setting. The external environment on the other hand, consists of all sub-sectors of the economy where the company operates. The company has no control over any of them. It can regulate factors within the company, for example, if the overhead is high, it can choose not to employ or lay-off some workers to reduce cost. It may buy new equipments to increase production efficiency or decides to change its suppliers. It may relocate to a more spacious location or another city. The following are beyond its control, at best the Management may succeed in influencing certain decisions of the government. This is probably the reason for forming trade pressure groups like the Chambers of Commerce and Industry to lobby and champion their course with the government functionaries.

Political/Government the political environment is very important to the survival of any business. A political stable country has the high propensity for flourishing business growth than unstable countries. Many of them are found in third world countries. Instability quickly cripples business, because nobody or investors will put his money in a country that is ridden in crisis. In a democratic society, there is a relative peace as there is a systematic change in the political gladiators. It should be noted that Government is a big buyer and their policies can also impinged on the success of business

Economy performance and survival of any business depends largely on the economy environment, which is considered to be the greatest. The pattern and impact of demand and supply is measured in its invisible hands that allocate scarce resources. The economy controls the variability of factors of production such as capital, quality and price of labor, the productivity output per man hour, the existing fiscal and monetary policies and other components that sum up the National Income. When economic boom, businesses boom any adverse effect on economy can spell doom for many businesses.

Law/Legal all countries of the world no matter the size have their legal system that must be obeyed. The body of rules and regulations are melt for individual and corporate citizens as well and since organization operates within such country any law that affect its operation may signal it continue existence. For instance a company the sell only sugar as it line of business. Once a law is passed that no more importation of such commodity, the company that rely on importation of sugar definitely seizes to exist. Company should always update itself with relevant laws to guide against be caught unaware or unprepared

Competitor this is a company that produces or render same as yours. Your competitors can chock you out of business if he produces better products and cheaper prices, if he uses modern technology and you still use equipments purchase in the last century. It will do everything possible to have your chuck of the market share, if it has everything it takes to push you behind the burner, it will not doubt use it against you. This confirm the unethical dictum, 'if you don't kill your competitor, your competitor will kill you'

Socio-Cultural customs, beliefs and tradition of the people are very important to an organization that strives to survival. Group's attitude, expectation and desire are closely monitored. For example, a company that deals with pork should note that is not good in Muslims community. Belief and attitude, no doubt, differs across social strata in the society and amongst races or ethnic. A company has to constantly monitor events in a complex society and do research on marketing.

Physical this is natural endowments such as Land, Water, and Air. Factories are built on land and most of the natural recourses are from the belly of the earth. Water is equally important for industry, oil and gas ridges are built on high seas. Some Industries need it for their production like the spring water, sodas or minerals etc. and Air is a mean of transportation at a fastest rate. Any problem on the above will affect the survival and profitability of an organization that depends on them.

Technology this is knowledge available on how things are done. In the last one decade, technology has taken a giant stride. Visually a manual job is being taken over by the use of technological equipments. Technology also includes inventions, techniques and the great influences on mankind. Today one can do everything on the internet. You can do shopping with a supplier in far away Middle East without knowing the supplier and may not meet him ever and the goods or service get to him in the USA faster and cheaper. If a USA based company produces the same products, expenses and takes week before getting to consumer in East Coast, it is done on the company that technology is edging it out of business. Company should be flexible to technological change of new products, new machines, new tools, new materials and new serves. Any company that allows technological change to over-takes its will produce obsolete products at high costs and still dances in old lyrics, while other are enjoying new lyrics

Suppliers these are company seller of raw materials needed to product final goods. They are very important for re-order level. They are as good as company's clients. They also provide trade credits that can be of help, when organization is cash strap. A continuous stream of supplies is needed to keep the industry moving and meet its customers demand. Must constantly be place of surveillance on the quantity of goods supply, the costs should not be increased arbitrarily and against competitors' attempt to lure him away.

Educations the quality of personnel, especially the management team are drawn from this vital sector. Old workforce, who are retiring are replaced by fresh human capital from education sub-sector. The qualities of sound managers are dependent on quality of graduates that this sector produces. New idea and new techniques are provided from the ivy towers across the county. The sector is what I wish to conveniently refer to as 'Finished Human Products'

Financial institutions this is another important sector make up of banks, insurance and other lenders. The sectors assist the company, when huge money is needed either to expand facility, retooling, and beef up working capital. It assists company to raise fund in the capital and money markets

The above are very important to an organization's survival and performance. They are the Concept of Relevant Environment that cannot be ignored. They must be taken into consideration by organization that wants to survive when taking decisions or formulating policies at any point in time.

9.2 TYPE OF BUSINESS

a. **Extracting:** This is concerned with all those industries that take/extract resources from the forest, mines, farms, seas/ oceans. These industries produce raw materials from which finished goods are made.

b. **Processing:** The business in this industry transform raw materials into various forms as requested by other industries.

c. **Manufacturing:** It consists industries that produce industrial and consumer goods processed from the raw materials to finished produces.

d. **Distribution:** The industries involve in physical movement of products from the producers to the title ownership or consumers.

e. **Services:** This is responsible for auxiliary activities vital to the survival of industries in the above sectors; examples of same industries are: Banking, Insurance, Shipping, Law, Accounting, Communications and so on. Industries in the Service sector of economy do rarely deal with physical products.

9.3 OBJECTIVES/GOALS OF AN INDUSTRY

Organization that engages in any of the above has the following objectives and goals. These are the reasons why organizations are in business

☐ Serve objective – A company must produce good products or provides excellence services. Serve must be the primary objective why companies should be in business

☐ Survival objective – A company is a pseudo person. Like human being its must strive to survive and remain in business for perpetually

☐ Growth objective – A company must not remain in the same 'height' it's should growth and develop both in assets and profitability

☐ Profit objective – people erroneously feel that the reason for a company is to make profit. The answer is no. in fact, this should be the last. Should the first three objectives are taken care of adequately; profit will naturally flow in like never ending stream.

9.4 BUSINESS ETHICS

The concept of business ethics is the type of general norms and conducts considered to be morally right or morally wrong. The norms that are acceptable and those that are not acceptable in practice from business organizations.

i. Business ethics demand that organization do not sell sub-standard or harmful goods to the public for consumption, even though customers heavily demand for such goods. It should be withdrawn from the market.

ii. Organizations do not bribe their ways to obtain trade secrets of their rivals or selling the trade secrets of their clients to a competitor.

iii. It is unethical for organization to offer kickbacks/bribes to enable it secure contracts.

iv. It is also unethical for an organization to engage in deceptive advertisement or publicity or promotion about its products and services.

v. In certain professions, it is frowned at and most unethical to lure away a key member of staff whom the company has heavily invested to acquire certain crucial skill that is in short supply.

vi. It is not only unethical but also criminal for organization to engage in industrial espionage.

Business can be formed or established to engage in any of the above. Below are types or categories of businesses, but must be registered in accordance with the law of the land where it wants to operate.

• Sole proprietor: this is a one man or woman 'show', where is formed and owned by a person. It also meant or said to be family business. It is not easily distinguishable or separated from its owner e.g. Aafin International LLC or Aafin Limited.

• Partnership: this is joint ownership by two or more persons. It has documents called Deeds of partnership that guides the conducts of members and stipulates the shares capital own by members as well as how profit and loss will be apportioned, distributed and shared

• Incorporated companies: This is separate legal entity different from the owners. This type of company can own properties, can sue and can be sued just like every individual.

   - Company limited by shares this can be closed/private, when their shares are not traded on the floor of Stock Exchange. It can be public, which means members of the public can own their shares or stocks

   - Company limited by Guarantee

   - Incorporated but unlimited example if Exxon-Mobil unlimited in Nigeria

• Mutual Association like the Co-operative society

9.5 TYPE OF CUSTOMERS

There are types of customers or clients that can make or mar companies and their products and services. Organizations should strive to identify them and apply appropriate strategy to tolerate them. The following are type of customers as categorized by Jones & Sasser.

Loyalist Customer: Customer is completely satisfied and keeps coming or returning.

Apostle Customer: Customer is so satisfied that he/she broadcasts the good news to everybody, everywhere and every time.

Defector Customer: Customer is satisfied, neutral and sometimes merely satisfied and has high defection tendency.

Terrorist Customer: Customer had a bad experience and broadcasts this with careless abandon. This is opposite of Apostle Customer.

Mercenary Customer: Customer is satisfied but shows no loyalty of sort, he/she is costly to attract and is quick to defect.

Hostage Customer: Customer patronizes because he/she has no choice, such as utility like electricity and water.

9.6 ORGANIC FUNCTIONS OF BUSINESS

Most businesses have four organic functions and work together to achieve organizational objectives. They are Production, Marketing, Finance and Personnel

a. Production function involves in production, services, manufacturing and assembly plant.
b. Services: are services that cannot be physically seen or touched like insurance, banking, transportation, law, accounting, auditing, management and they are auxiliaries vital function and connective tissues of Business System
c. Manufacturing: converting raw or semi-raw materials into finished products through chemical or mechanical processes into finished products. It engages in mass production in order to meet customers or job order and process production.
d. Assembly are mostly in plant that assembly various components from two or more firms for example the Ford Auto Assembly Plant or Toyota plant in Japan or Peugeot plant in Nigeria and France. The plant takes input for auto manufacturer parts like the seats, glass, radios, navigation systems etc, which they don't manufacture by themselves.

2. Marketing is very crucial for any products and services. Products are not manufactured for decoration in the company. This function pushes these products and services to the final consumers. It advertises them and promotes the products and services. It feels the impulse of the markets and brings feedbacks.

3. Finance source and provides funds at all levels. The raw materials must be paid for; the goods have to be moved to the markets. The finance source for funds in an efficient manner from banks, financial institutions and make it available to various units including workers salaries and wages.

4. Personnel are the human capital that is needed to make the differences. Without human effort none of the above function will work. Personnel are recruited to work in various departments, units and sections. They are trained and developed to fit into a particular need of each department. They are recruited in such a way there is no over staff or under staff. The rewards in exchange for their effort must be balanced otherwise such company will lose them to its competitors.

CHAPTER TEN

THE LEADERSHIP

10.1 LEADERSHIP CONCEPT

Leadership although mentioned earlier, but because of its importance in the life of the leadership and the lead will be treated separately in this chapter. Leadership cut across all disciplines and is the most controversial and perilous sub-set in management. Leadership has substantial and large in any society and particularly the influence its weight in an organization. Although, it belongs to such concept that people refuse to reach a consensus as to who is a leader, his roles and his followers. While the myth surrounding it is being sorted out, it is believed that leadership is the act of leading other people. His functions include but not limited to controlling human and materials resources to achieve a common goal. He engages in all functions of Management of planning, organizing, coordinating, directing, controlling, staffing and budgeting. In an organization leadership has been described as sub-set of management, the umbrella concept.

10.2 DEFINITION OF LEADERSHIP:

While like Management itself, leadership has no catholic definition, but Mc Farland (1979), Davis and Newton (1985) have provided working definitions into the subject matter. Leadership is the ability of an individual to influence others to work beyond his ordinary level to achieve goal and Leadership is the process of helping others to work enthusiastically towards objects respectively.

10.3 LEADERSHIP THEORIES

There are three major leadership theories namely:
Trait or Great Man Theory: this is the oldest and is believed that leaders are born and not made. Those in this school believe leadership is in-born and that it is natural and not nurtured. It is hereditary and not contingent upon an environmental instinct. It made it clear that you cannot acquire the act of leadership except you are born with it. It went further that once you are born and have royal blood in you, will be automatically be a leader.

The recent experiences have proved this theory wrong, where someone without the spell of dynasty performed well and is great leaders.

Behavioral Theory: studies conducted by the Ohio, Iowa and Michigan Leadership Schools in the USA reveal that leaders' behavior and interaction with his followers have either shaped or marred the organizational fortune. Some leaders' emphasis on task accomplishments or productivity, while other leaders' emphasis on group maintenance and concern for people he leads. None of these are that bad altogether, but leaders with concern for his followers and balance it with tasks are better leaders than mechanistic leader, who is only interested in getting the job done as if his followers are machines.

Contingency or Situational or All Depends Theory: It is so called these because the act of Manager depends of circumstance and situation on hand. For instance, when a decision is to be taken take as quickly as possible. It will be unwise for the Manager to call meetings and debate and possibly voting, before all the bureaucracy is completed the business might have gone down the drain. That is why the Chief Executive Officer sometimes takes critical decisions; failure to act immediately might affect the company's fortune adversely. He however comes back to the Board of Directors for ratification if the act is above his strength of authority.

The New Leadership Theories: As a result of observations, studies and hypothesis new leadership theories have emerged such as the Styles theories (autocratic, Democratic and Laissez Faire), others are Aggressive theory, Charismatic theory, Transactional theory and Transformational theory.

10.4 LEADERSHIP STYLES

This has led us to the styles leadership in other to achieve their goals and objectives. There are three styles.

Autocratic or Authoritarian: leader acquires and holds to his/her chest all decisions, while consultations whatsoever with anybody except himself. He is so dogmatic that solutions to problems reside only with him. He uses threats, force and very coercive, dribbles, and highly manipulative. He is benevolent and uses carrot in hand, pat on the back and stick to wipe the buttocks to achieve his aim at all costs. Decision is taken as quickly as possible, which minimizes delay.

Democratic or Participative: The leaders sees himself not having the monopoly of knowledge and so shares decisions with his sub-ordinates. He reaches out to his followers before reaching any decisions. He makes them feels they are involve and raises their ego and bolster their motivations. Decisions are usually delay especially where many sub-ordinates to be consulted.

Laissez-Faire: instead of making decision by leader, he or she passes it to his or sub-ordinated by adjudicating his role. He will re-join the group as a member. He passes responsibilities and decision making process to sub-ordinate there entrusting high degree of freedom. Decision is not only very slow, but an invitation to chaos and some over-zealous sub-ordinate us the unique opportunity to rain havoc. In other to perfect the deed of a Leader in his working relationship with his subordinates, various approaches are propounded by individual or group of individuals such as the Strategy Approach, the Human-Assets approach, The Expertise, The Box approach and the Change Approach

However, of all the about leadership styles, none is the best and none is worst, it only depend on situation and circumstances the leader finds himself. There are many factors that can influence the degree of effectiveness of a leader, especially if the size of the organization is large and complex. The leaders will be operating at a turbulent and high dynamo and explosive situation. If the leader works in an environment, where members of the group are united, loving, and work together harmoniously, things will be much easier for the leader. Personal attributes and qualities of the leader like technical know-how, competence, agility, energetic, vitality, empathy, sound communication and human relations skills, emotional stability, objectivity, leading by example, ability to inspire his followers, mental alertness and motivational dispositions will enable him/her successful, but no human is such a super being that can possess all the above. He needs Devine guardian to be able to water the storm and run a prosperous company.

10.5 MANAGEMENT BEHAVIOUR

MBO	-	Management By Objective (Peter Drucker)
MBE	-	Management By Exception (F. W. Taylor)
MBC	-	Management By Coercion
MBI	-	Management By Intimidation
MBCf	-	Management By Confrontation
MBEx	-	Management By Example
MBP	-	Management By Participation (Mary P. Follett)
MBD	-	Management By Drive
MBM	-	Management By Motivation
MBDi	-	Management By Dictation
MBPe	-	Management By Persuasion
MBDe	-	Management By Delegation
MBT	-	Management By Threat (sack or give query)
MBS	-	Management By Submission
MBDec	-	Management By Deceit
MBSe	-	Management By Settlement
MBSi	-	Management By Simplicity
MBR	-	Management By Repression
MBSu	-	Management By Suppression
MBOp	-	Management By Oppression.
MBMa	-	Management By Manipulation
MBF	-	Management By Force
MBCo	-	Management By Committee
MBP	-	Management By Prescription

GLOSSARY

Administrator: A person who has responsibility for implementing the aims and objectives in an organization e.g. Universities, Hospitals.

Attitude: Manner that shows the expression of an action.

Authority: The right to do something as entrusted by higher authority in an organization.

Behavioral Science: Is the scientific study of human behavior in all its ramifications. It is an applied science that:
- Under-studies human behavior
- Explains human behavior
- Predicts human behavior
- Controls human behavior

Behavioral science has individual level, group level, organizational level and societal level. It also uses the following disciplines.

a. PSYCHOLOGY: The scientific study of behavior of man and animals for the purpose of understanding their similarity, how they are different and why they are different

b. SOCIOLOGY: The study of group behavior, its structure, function and processes. There are three types; study of groups, study of social situations for example marriage, kingship and the study of structure.

c. ANTHROPOLOGY: Is science of man. It is divided into two types: (i) Physical Anthropology; this is the area Behavioral Science interprets and (ii) Cultural Anthropology; the study of the original history of man's creation.

Budget: This is a statement of expected result express in numerical terms. It is a controlling device, which has a time limit.

Collegial: A spirit of teamwork and partnership amongst the employees in respect to the objective and exercising power in an organization.

Corporate Planning: Setting organizational goals and objectives for a period of time. It is a term to denote a formal, comprehensive and systematic appraisal of internal and environmental factors.

Corporate Strategy: A set of unifying and comprehensive goals.
***De Facto*:** Where authority is usurped, that is, bottom-up authority.
***De Jure*:** Formally delegated authority from top bottom.

Delegation: Process where the individual manager or super-ordinate transfers part of his legitimate authority to a subordinate.

Drive: It is an energizer of behavior or response.
Ecosystem: The relationship between an organization and its environment. They both need support for one another.

Employment: A contractual agreement between employee and employer by which the former earns an income.

Entrepreneur: One, who perceives, evaluates, mobilizes and takes action/ steps in bringing resources to actualization.

Goal: What an organization sets out to achieve in a short run, using all resources at its disposal.

Grapevine: An informal communication channels in an organization.

Hypothesis: A set of propositions to explain the occurrence group of phenomena.

Informal Group: A group of people coming together with a common interest/purpose to their own advantage.

Integration/Diversification: This is a commonly used term by organizational strategists. It is the unification of a number of successive or similar operations e.g. combination of companies, a company taking over of a portion of an industrial/commercial process previously accomplishes by other firm. Thus:

- Vertical/Forward Integration/Diversification: This is integration towards the final users of company goods and services i.e. a company distributing its own products.
- Backward Integration/Diversification: When a company controls the source of input including raw materials/labor
- Horizontal Integration/Diversification: Buying or taken control of competitors in the same industry at the same level in production/marketing process, thereby enjoying economy of scale.
- Lateral /Sideway Integration/Diversification: It involves integrating with other company in different industries to expand turnover, acquire techniques, skills and other inputs.

Management: A group of managers who occupy the upper most echelon of an organization with overall responsibility of planning, decision making, establishing goals, formulating policies and strategies towards achieving organization's stated goals for example, the Management of Aafin Limited.

Mission: A statement outlines an organization's business objective. It is comprehensive and futuristic as to where an organization wishes to be and achieve in future.

Needs: The initiating and sustaining forces of behavior, which helps to dictate actions.

Objective: This is the direction in which an organization is going in a long run.

Parkinson's Law: Developed by North Cote c. Parkinson to explain wasteful practices in an organization.

Personality: Totality of one's psychological characteristics e.g. motives, drives, intelligence, needs, traits with which he/she relates to people.

Policy: General statements that guide decision making or a guide to an action. In specific term, it is a guide to managerial action.

Power: Ability to do something.

Principle: Guideline to enable one formulates theory.

Procedures: They are customary ways of dealing with recurring events in a uniform manner. It provides chronological, systematical sequence and more specific guidance to achieve goals and objectives. It is narrower than policies.

Programme: Detailed number of proceeding of what to do, steps to be taken when carrying out a given course of action.

Purpose: The reason why an organization is in business.

Research: It is investigation or experimentation undertaken to establish facts.

Responsibility: The obligation to do something when he or she accepts an assignment.

Rules and Regulations: Specific and definite statements/actions to be taken and what boundaries of acceptable behavior are.

Strategy: A company's overall planning that determines the kind of result envisage in its environment.

Strategy Management: A process of determining the long run direction and performance of an organization by unifying all its parts.

Strategy Planning: An orderly process of determining organizational goals and objectives. It is long term in nature.

SMART: An acronym use for target setting, that is, Specific, Measurable, Achievable, Realizable and Time bound.

SWOT/WOTS: An acronym for Strength, Weakness, Opportunity and Threat.

Synergy: The whole is greater than the sum of its parts such that 2 + 1 = 5 or more.

Theory: It is a body of principles that guide a coherent and systematic group of inter-dependent concepts and principles, which give a framework to or tie together significant knowledge. It is a scientific formation useful in understanding/explaining relationship between two or more observable facts or events or phenomena and use to predict future happenings.

APPENDICES

APPENDIX A

MANAGEMENT GURUS

Abraham Maslow
Adam Smith
Adrian Furnham
Alfred Chandler
Anthony Athos
Aristotle Armand Feigenbaum
Art Kleiner
Bruce Henderson
Charles Babbage
Chester Barnard
Chris Argyris
Christopher Bartlett
Clayton P. Alderfer
Coimbatore Krishnarao Prahalad
Dale Carnegie
David Norton
Donald Shön
Douglas McGregor
Edwards Deming
Elton Mayo
Emerson Harrington
Emile Durkheim
Frank and Lillian Gilbreth
Fred Edward Fiedler
Frederick Taylor
Gary Hamel
Geert Hofstede
Henri Fayol
Henry Gantt
Igor Ansoff
James Champy

Abraham Maslow

Abraham (Harold) Maslow (April 1, 1908 June 8, 1970) was an American psychologist. Maslow is mostly noted today for his proposal of a hierarchy of human needs and is considered the father of humanistic psychology.

Adam Smith

Adam Smith was a Scottish moral philosopher and a pioneering political economist. One of the key figures of the intellectual movement known as the Scottish Enlightenment, he is known primarily as the author of two treatises: The Theory of Moral Sentiments (1759), and An Inquiry into the Nature and Causes of the Wealth of Nations (1776).

Chris Argyris

Chris Argyris, adult education/organizational behavior expert and Professor Emeritus at the Harvard Graduate Schools of Business and Education. Argyris originally graduated in psychology, economics and organizational behavior from Yale and went on to produce many books and seminars in the area of Learning Organizations.

Donald Shön

Donald Shön was a philosopher and progressive thinker

James David Thompson
James MacGregor Burns
Jay Lorsch
Joan Woodward
Johannes M. Pennings
John Adair
Joseph Juran
Kaoru Ishikawa
Kenichi Ohmae
Kurt Lewin
Luther Gulick
Lyndall Urwick
Machiavelli
Mary Parker Follett
Max Weber
Meredith Belbin
Michael Hammer
Michael Porter
Paul Lawrence
Peter Blau
Peter Drucker
Philip Crosby
Rensis Likert
Robert K. Merton
Robert Kaplan
Robert Owen
Socrates
Sumantra Ghoshal
Sun Tzu
Tom Peters
Vilfredo Pareto
Warren Bennis
William Ouchi
Xenophon

whose development into the theory and practice of reflective and professional learning has been applied to a wide range of business fields.

David Norton

Dr. David P. Norton is co-author, with Dr. Robert S Kaplan, of The Execution Premium: Linking Strategy to Operations for Competitive Advantage, his fifth Balanced Scorecard book. David P. Norton is founder and president of Renaissance Strategy Group, a consulting firm located in Lincoln, Massachusetts.

William Ouchi

William Ouchi first came to prominence for his studies of the differences between Japanese and American companies and management styles. His first popular book Theory Z in 1981 summarized his observations.

Vilfredo Pareto

An Italian economist and sociologist, known for his application of mathematics to economic analysis and for his theory of the 'circulation of elites'. Vilfredo Pareto was the father of the concept of "social systems"

CHRONOLOGY OF CONTRIBUTORS TO MANAGEMENT THEORIES, DATES AND AFFILIATED INSTITUTIONS

1770s
- Adam Smith   University of Glasgow

1800s
- Robert Owen   New Lanark, Scotland Textile Mills
- Charles Babbage   Cambridge University
- Henry V. Poor   American Railroad Journal
- Daniel McCallum   Erie Railroad
- William S. Jevons   University College, London
- Henry R. Towne   Yale and Towne Manufacturing Co
- Henry Metcalfe   Frankford Arsenal
- Boulton & Watt   Soho Engineering Foundry

1900s
- Frederick W. Taylor   Midvale Steel Company
- Henry L. Gantt   Midvale Steel Company
- Frank B. Gilbreth   Whidden and Company
- Max Weber   University of Frelburg

1910s
- Henri Fayol   S. A. Commentry-Fourchambault
- Lillian M. Gilbreth   Independent Consultant
- Harrington Emerson   Independent Consultant
- Harlow S. Person   Dartmouth College
- Morris L. Cooke   City of Philadelphia, Pa.
- Robert Hoxie   University of Chicago
- Mary Parker Follett   Independent Consultant
- Chester Irving Barnard   New Jersey Bell Telephone Co.
- James D. Mooney   General Motors Corporation
- Alan C. Reiley   General Motors Corporation
- V.A. Graicunas   Independent Consultant

- Elton Mayo   Harvard University
- Fritz J. Roethlisberger   Harvard University
- William J. Dickson   Western Electric Company

1940s
- Lyndall F. Urwick   Urwick, Orr and Partners
- Ralph C. Davis   Ohio State University
- Herbert A. Simon   Carnegie-Mellon University
- Kurt Lewin   Massachusetts Institute of
                                    Technology

1950s
- Peter Drucker   Claremont, Califonia
- Chris Argyris   Yale University
- Ralph M. Stogdill   Ohio State University
- Harold Koontz   University of California, LA
- Cyril O'Donnell   University of California, LA
- William H. Newman   Columbia University
- Sune Carlson   University College of
                                    Commerce, Stockhol
- Rensis Likert   University of Michigan
- James G. March   Carnegie-Mellon University
- Douglas McGregor   Massachusetts Institute of
                                    Technology

1960s
- Richard A. Johnson   University of Washington
- Fremont E. Kast   University of Washington
- James E. Rosenzweig   University of Washington
- Dan Voich   Florida State University
- Daniel A. Wren   Florida State University
- Harry C. Triandis   University of Illinois
- Paul R. Lawrence   Harvard University
- Jay W. Lorsch   Harvard University
- Ernest Dale   Cornell University
- Michelon L. C.   Republic Steel Corporation

- William T. Greenwood — Southern Illinois University
- Bertram M. Gross — Syracuse University
- Justin G. Longenecker — Baylor University
- Joseph L. Massie — University of Kentucky
- Charles E. Summer — Columbia University
- Kirby E. Warren — Columbia University
- John K. Hemphill — Educational Testing Service
- Bernard Berelson — The Population Council
- Gary A. Steiner — University of Chicago
- James L. Price — University of Iowa
- James D. Thompson — Indiana University
- Warren G. Bennis — Massachusetts Institute of Technology
- Richard Cyert — Carnegie-Mellon University

1970s

- Fred Luthan
- William Ouchi
- David C. McClelland
- Robert J. House
- Clayton P. Alderfer
- Hugo Munsterberg
- Keith Davis
- Harold J. Leavitt
- Phillip W. Yetton
- Huse E.F.
- Phillip B. Crosby

1980s

- Ishikawa Kaoru
- Joseph Juran
- Edward W. Deming
- Rosemary Stewart

1990s

- John R. Adair

APPENDIX B

MANAGEMENT SCHOOLS AND AUTHORS

Administrative management

Administrative management focuses on how a business should be organized and the practices an effective manager should follow. The two major contributors to administrative management school of thought were Henri Fayol (1930) and Max Weber (1922).

Bureaucratic Management

Bureaucratic management may be described as "a formal system of organization based on clearly defined hierarchical levels and roles in order to maintain efficiency and effectiveness." Max Weber embellished the scientific management theory with his bureaucratic management theory.

Neoclassical School

As a reaction to schools of classical theory which over-emphasized the mechanical and physiological characters of Management came up the schools of neoclassical theory with more human oriented approach and focus on time needs, drives, behaviors and attitudes of individuals.

[1] CLASSICAL/ UNIVERSAL/TRADITIONAL/MANAGEMENT PROCESS SCHOOL

I. CLASSICAL THEORY:

a)   Administrative Theory:

- Arkwright Richard
- Babbage Charles   1832
- Davis R. C.   1961
- Dinne Earnest   1959
- Fayol Henri (Leader)   1916
- Gulick Luther   1930
- Luthan Fred.   1977
- Mooney James. D.   1931
- Newman H. William   1961
- O'Donnes Cyril   1968
- Owen Robert   1858
- Reiley C. Alan
- Salomon Herber   1945
- Sloam A. D.   1938
- Summer C.E. Jr   1961
- Terry Judge   1967
- Urwick F. Lyndal   1937

(b)   Bureaucratic

- Adams J. Stacy   1963
- Durkheim Emile
- Festinger Sigmud Feud leo   1963
- Webber Max (Leader)   1921

II. SCIENTIFIC MANAGEMENT THEORY:

- Barth Carl Georg
- Boulton M.   1800
- Brandies D. Louis
- Emerson E. Harrington   1931

- Filene A. Edward
- Frederick Hasley
- Gantt L. Henry — 1919
- Gilberth Bunker Frank — 1924
- Gilberth Moller Lillian — 1972
- Harlow S. Person
- Jevons S. William
- Morris L. Cooke
- Taylor F. Winslow (Leader) — 1911
- Towne Henry
- Watt James — 1800

[2] BEHAVIOURAL/HUMAN BEHAVIOUR/HUMAN RELATIONS SCHOOL

- Abraham H. Maslow — 1954
- Adair R. John — 1990
- Alderfer P. Clayton — 1972
- Argyris Chris — 1964
- Atkinso W. John
- Bakke Wight
- Beach S. Dale — 1975
- Blake R. Robert — 1964
- Churchman C. West
- Dale Ernest — 1960
- Dalton Gen. W. — 1970
- Davis and Newton — 1985
- Davis Keith — 1972
- Dickson William — 1967
- Drucker Peter — 1950
- Dubin Robert — 1974
- Fillery C. Alan — 1978
- Follett Mary Parker — 1933
- Herzberg Frederick — 1966
- Homans G. C.
- House J. Robert — 1971
- Koontz Harold — 1961
- Lawler III E. E. — 1968

- Leavitt J. Harold   1972
- Lewin Kurt   1947
- Likert Rennis   1967
- Lyman W. Porter
- Mayo E. George (Leader)   1946
- McClelland C. David   1971
- McFarland   1979
- McGregor M. Douglas   1969
- Mouton S. Jane   1964
- Munsterberg Hugo   1975
- Murray A. Henry
- Norbert Wiener
- Ouchi William   1972
- Pareto Vilfredo   1917
- Peter J. Laurence   1969
- Peters Thomas   1982
- Roethlisberger J. Fritz   1983
- Routree B. Seebohm
- Sayles R. Leonard   1966
- Schein H. Edgar   1970
- Scott Dill Walter   1911
- Selznick Phillip   1968
- Sheldon Oliver   1951
- Silverman D.   1978
- Steiner A. George
- Tannenbaum Robert   1961
- Stogdill Ralph
- Vroom H. Victor   1947
- Warren G. Bennis   1966
- Waterman Robert   1982
- Yetton W. Phillip   1973
- Zaleznik Abraham   1966

[3] MANAGEMENT SCIENCE / QUANTITATIVE SCHOOL

- Mathematicians
- Physicists

- Scientists
- Shewhart A. Walter   1931
- Whitney Eli

[4] SYSTEM SCHOOL

- Barnard Chester Irving   1938
- Bertalanffy Von Ludwig
- Boulding E. Kenneth   1966
- Huse E. F.   1979
- Kahn R. L.   1966
- Katz Daniel   1966
- March G. James.   1958
- Simon A. Herber   1958

[5] CONTINGENCY / SITUATIONAL / ALL DEPENDS / REVISIONIST SCHOOL:

- Burns Tom   1966
- Fielder E. Fielder   1967
- Lawrence Paul   1968
- Lorsch W. Jay   1968
- Massie L. Joseph
- Stalker G. M.   1966
- Stewart Rosemary   1982
- Woodward Joan   1958

[6] TOTAL QUALITY MANAGEMENT [TQM]

- Croby Phillip B.   1975
- Deming Edward (Leader)   1986
- Feigenbaum V. Armand   1960
- Ishikawa Kaoru   1982
- Juran Joseph   1989
- MacArthur Gen. Douglas   1950

- Shewhat W. A.   1920
- Taguchi Genichi   1960

Some of the above classifications are based on Prof. Harold Koontz's "Management Theory Classified" (1961) and Claude S. George Jr. "The History of Management Thought" (1972).

APPENDIX C

MANAGEMENT THEORIES

14 Principles of Management
3 Dim. of Strategic Change
3C's Model of Kenichi Ohmae
7-S Framework of McKinsey
80-20 rule
Action Centered Leadership
Adam Smith Problem
ADL Matrix
Ansoff Matrix
Balanced Scorecard
BCG Matrix
Benchmarking
Benefit-Cost Analysis - BCA
Blue Ocean Strategy
Bricks and Clicks Model
Business Process Reengineering
Capability Maturity Model
CMM
Clarkson Principles
Competitive Advantage
Competitive Advantage of
Nations
Core Competencies
Core Group Theory
Cost-Benefit Analysis
Cultural Dimensions
Delta Model
Deming Cycle
Deming's 14 Points
Diamond Model
DRIFT Theory
ERG Theory
Experience Curve
Extended marketing mix 7ps
Fiedler's Contingency Model
Fishbone Diagram
Five Forces of Competition
Force Field Analysis
Game Theory

Pareto Chart

A Pareto chart is a special type of bar chart where the values being plotted are arranged in descending order. The chart is named after Vilfredo Pareto, and its use in quality assurance was popularized by Joseph M. Juran and Kaoru Ishikawa.

Quality Circles

The concept behind quality circles is widely believed to have been developed in Japan in 1962 by Kaoru Ishikawa as a method to improve quality, though it is also argued that the practice started with the United States Army soon after 1945, whilst restoring the war torn nation, and the Japanese adopted and adapted the concept and its application.

Gantt Chart
GE Matrix of McKinsey
Greiner Growth Curve
Hawthorne Effect
Ishikawa Diagram
Lewin's Leadership Styles
Linking Pin Model
M-Form Society
M-Shape Society
Maslow's Hierarchy of Needs
Organizational Learning
Pareto Chart
Pareto Principle
PDCA
Porter's Five Forces
Porter's Competitive Strategies
POSDCORB
Product Market Grid
Quality Circles
Socratic Problem
Strategy Delta
Team Role Model
Theory U
Theory X and Y
Theory Z
Twelve Principles of Efficiency
Wealth of Nations
Weighing-Scale Approach

LIKELY EXAMINATON Q & A

QUESTIONS:

1.   Management may be defined as Art, Process, Function, Concept, Profession, Science and Intuition.
True/False

2.   Modern history of management can be traced to the following:-
(a) Post World War II
(b) Industrial revolution
(c) Kiriji War
(d) Nigerian civil war
(e) Post-Machiavellian period
(f) Pre-colonial period.

3.   ....coined management theory jungle
(a) Dr. J.U.J. Onwumere
(b) Dr. M.A. Aluko
(c) Prof. Gullick
(d) Prof. Hugo Munsterberg
(e) Prof. Harold Koontz
(f) Mr. Henri Fayol

4.   The other name of Classical School is?
(a) Scientific Management School
(b) Bureaucratic Approach
(c) Universal School
(d) Administrative Approach
(e) Non of the above

5.   The Classical School is divided into two approaches namely and...

6.   Which of the following is regarded as leader of administrative approach?
(a) Chester I. Bernard
(b) Charles Babbage
(c) Rennis Liker
(d) Henri Fayol
(e) F.W. Taylor

7.   The mechanical calculator was refer to as...... and was invented by.....

8.   The management theorist who developed the concept of Bureaucracy was
(a) Robert Owen
(b) Carl Barth
(c) Mary P. Follett
(d) Peter Drucker
(e) Douglas McGregor
(f) Max Webber

9.   Dissonance Theory of motivation was developed by
(a) Emile Durkheim
(b) Adam J. Stacy
(c) Sigmund Feud Leo Festinger
(d) Summee C. E.
(e) Davis R.C.

10.   Scientific Management Theory leader who rose through the ranks to become Chief Executive Engineer is
(a) Robert L. Katz
(b) Fritz Roethlisberger
(c) Fredrick Winslow Taylor
(d) William Dickson
(e) G. M. Stalker

11.   ....was widely acclaimed as the 'First Lady' of management
a) Mary Parker Follett
(b) Rachael Olubola
(c) Lillian M. Gilbreth

(d) Joan Woodward
(e) Rosemary Stewart

12.   The Classical Management Theory's contributions to the study of management are based on............and............

13.   Scientific Management is also called
    (a) Standardization approach
    (b) Wages approach
    (c) Productivity approach
    (d) High pay approach
    (e) Rule of thumb

14.   The leader of famous Hawthorne studies is
    (a) John R. Adair
    (b) Sayles r. Leonard
    (c) Thomas Peter
    (d) Elton Mayo
    (e) Seebohm B. Rouee
    (f) Robert Waterman

15.   ....developed Existence, Relatedness and Growth theory of theory of motivation, which is a compressed/merger of Abraham Maslow's five hierarchies of needs?
    (a) Abraham Zaleznik
    (b) William Ouchi
    (c) David C. McClelland
    (d) Douglas M. McGregor
    (e) Clayton P. Alderfer
    (f) Chris Argyris

16.   A French-Italian scholar who is regarded as the father of Social System approach to organization and management is?
    (a) Blake R. Robert
    (b) Lawrence Peter
    (c) Walter Dill Scott
    (d) Dubin Robert
    (e) Robert Tannenbaum
    (f) Harold J. Leavitt

(g) Vilfredo Pareto

17.   Who is the father of Industrial Psychology and efficiency who developed managerial roles?

(a) Norbert Weiner
(b) Dalton Gen. W
(c) Henry A. Murray
(d) Hugo Munsterberg
(e) Ernest Dale
(f) John W. Atkinso

18.   Operations Research, System Analysis, Quantitative Approach, System Science, Quantitative Approach, System Science, Quantitative Analysis, Decision Science, Analysis for Decision Making are names for which school
(a) Human Relations
(b) Scientific Management
(c) System School
(d) Situational/Contingency
(e) Management Science
(f) Total Quality Management

19.   The sequential evolution of management theories can be arranged as follows:
(a) System, Contingency, Quantitative, Universal, TQM, Human Relations,
(b) Universal, Human Relations, Quantitative, System, TQM, Contingency.
(c) TQM, Universal, Human Relations, Quantitative, Contingency, System.
(d) Contingency, Universal, Human Relations, System, TQM, Quantitative
(e) Universal, Human Relations, Quantitative, System, Contingency, TQM.

20..   A system operating without exchange from outside is referred to as:
(a) Negative Entropy
(b) Feedback
(c) Equifinality

(d) Differentiation

(e) Closed System

(f) Dynamic Homeostatic.

21.   The duo that developed system model that represent an organization as open system are:

(a) Mouton S. Jane & Robert R. Blake   (

b) Frank Bunker Gilbreth & Lillian M. Gilbreth

(c) D. Katz & R. L. Kahn

(d) Herber A. Simon & James G. March.

22.   Under Contingency School, Tom Burns propounded Mechanistic model that developed Organic Approach

(a) Jossy Nkwocha

(b) F. E. Fiddler

(c) Lawrence & Lorsch,

(d) G. M. Stalker

(e) Rosemary Stewart

(f) Margaret Nyamse

23.   TQM can be regarded as, which position in the sequential arrangement of schools of management

(a) Second

(b) fourth

(c) Current

(d) Sixth

(e) fifth

(f) First

(g) none of the above

24.   ………… can be regarded as the father of TQM

(a) General Douglas MacArthur

(b) Stewart W. A.

(c) Kaoru Ishikawa

(d) Dr. Edward W. Deming

(e) Dr. Joseph M. Juran

25.   Total Quality Management is

(a) Nigerian Management Philosophy

(b) Japanese Management Philosophy
(c) Western World Management Philosophy
(d) American Management Philosophy
(f) New Management Philosophy

26.   Types of business are ....,..., ... & ....

27.   Objectives / Goals of an industry are ....,........ & ....

28.   The first step in planning process is
(a) Goal Setting
(b) Environmental Scanning
(c) Select course of action
(d) Forecasting
(e) Develop alternative
(f) Select best alternative

29.   .... is not widely used method when forecasting
(a) Market Survey
(b) Time Series
(c) Gantt Chart
(d) Hunches
(e) Econometric

30.   An organization can be defined as:
(a) a social system
(b) a cultural structure
(c) a functional structure
(d) administrative structure
(e) A, B & C.

31.   The three skills developed by Robert L. Katz are:
(a) ....,
(b) Human Relations Skill and
(c) ....

32.   The efficiency and effectiveness of manager as defined by Peter Drucker are:
(a) Effectiveness .... and

(b) Efficiency ....

33.   The highly publicized Organizational Development Techniques was developed by .... and ....

34.   The managerial grid shows diagrammatic presentation of various leadership styles. Complete the following missing words or figures
(a) .... =   Impoverished Management
(b) 1, 9   = ... Management
(c) .... =   Task Management
(d)............ =   Middle of the road Management and
(e) 9, 9   = ... Management

35.   The three basic leadership styles are
(a) Participative
(b) Democratic
(c) Revisionist
(d) Authoritarian
(e) a, c & d
(f) b, c & d

36.   Below are steps in Decision making
(a) Identification of problem
(b) Development of alternative
(c) Deciding on the alternative
(d) Implementation of alternative chosen
(e) Follow up.

True or False

37.   Supply the missing steps and what should be their position(s) in question 36 above

38.   The acronym "POSDCORB" was an expansion of Fayol's elements /function of management. Who expanded it?
(a) Prof. Harold Koontz
(b) Prof. Luthan Gulick
(c) Prof. W. F. Glueck
(d) Prof. J. A. T. Ojo
(e) Prof. Cyril O'Donnell

39.   One of the definitions of management is the universality of its concept. The different in its application is called.
   (a) Management by objective
   (b) Management by Exemption
   (c) Intuitive Management
   (d) Cultural Management
   (e) Participative Management

40.   The grouping of views of founders or proponents of related/similar problems in management is called

ANSWERS:
   1. False
   2. B
   3. E
   4. C
   5. Administrative and Bureaucratic approaches
   6. D
   7. Deferent Machine and Prof. Charles Babbage
   8. F
   9. C
   10. C
   11. C
   12. Functional activities and what managers do in an organization
   13. C
   14. D
   15. E
   16. G
   17. D
   18. E
   19. E
   20. E
   21. C
   22. D
   23. D
   24. D
   25. D

26. Extracting, Processing, Manufacturing, Distribution and Services
27. Serve, Survival, Growth and Profit
28. A
29. C
30. E
31. Conceptual and Technical Skills
32. Do things right and Do right thing
33. Robert Blake and Jane Mouton
34. (a) 1, 1 (b) Country Club Management (c) 9, 1 (d) 5, 5 (e) Democratic Management
35. F
36. False
37. Evaluation of alternative no 3 and Feedback no. 7
38. B
39. D
40. School of Thought

BIBLIOGRAPHY

ACHUMBA, I. C. & Osuagwu L. C. (1994), <u>Marketing Fundamentals and Practice,</u> Lagos: Mukugamu Nigeria Limited.

ADAIR, John R. (1990), <u>Understanding Motivation. Survey:</u> The Talbot Adair Press.

ADAMS, J. Stacy, (1963), "Towards an understanding of inequity", <u>Journal of Abnormal & Social Psychology</u> 67: 422 to 424.

ADETULE, R. B. (1996), <u>The relationship between leadership style and employees performance,</u> Lagos: Parb Communications.

AGBATO, J. O. (1982), <u>Nature of Management; a text for Professionals,</u> Lagos

AKOMOLAFE, S. I. (1996), <u>The application of the marketing concept to Commercial Banking Services,</u> Lagos: Komo Communications.

AKPOYOMARE B. (1991), <u>Introduction to Management,</u> Lagos: Panaf Press

ALDERFER C. P. (1972), <u>Existence, Relatedness & Growth: Human Needs in organizational Setting,</u> N.Y: Free Press.

ALLEN C. Bluedorn, (1982): "Special Review Section on the Classics of Management" <u>Academy of Management Review</u> ed. PP442-464.

ALUKO, M. A. (1996), "Notes on Management"

ARGYRIS, Chris (1971): <u>Management & Organizational Development, the Path from XA to BY,</u> New York: McGraw

ASIKA Nnamdi (1988), <u>Motivational Characteristics of Financial Rewards in Nigeria,</u> Lagos: Hill Industries.

BARNARD, Chester Irving (1938), <u>The function of the Executive</u>, Cambridge, Mass.   Harvard University Press.

BEACH, Dale S. (1975), <u>Managing People at Work: Readings in person, 2nd Ed.</u> N.Y. Macmillan.

BEDEIAN G. Arthur & W. F. Glueck, (1983): <u>Management</u>, CBS College Publishing.

BENNIS, Warren G. (1966), <u>Leadership and Motivation</u>, Cambridge.

BENNIS, Warren G. (1990), <u>Why Leadership cannot lead: the unconscious conspiracy continues,</u> San Francisco: Jossy-bass publication.

BLAKE, R. R. & Jane S. Mouton, (1964), <u>The Managerial Grid</u>, Houston: Gulf Publishing Company

BOULDING, Kenneth E. (1966), <u>Economic Analysis 4th Ed.</u> N.Y.: Harper & Row.

BURNS, Tom & G. M. Stalker (1966), <u>Management of Innovation</u>, London: Tavistock.

BURNS, Tom & G. M. Stalker (1969), <u>Industrial Man</u>, Harmodsworth: Penguin

CROSBY Phillip B. and Taguchi, Crosby: (1979), <u>Quality is free</u>, The McGraw-Hill Book Company.

DALE, Ernest (1960), <u>The great Organizers</u>, NY: McGraw-Hill Co. Inc. PP 11-28.

DAVIS, Keith, (1972), <u>Human Behavior at Work: Human Relations and Organizational Behavior</u>, 4th ed. N.Y.: McGraw-Hill.

DEMING, Edward W. (1986), <u>Out of crisis,</u> Cambridge: MIT Press (p171)

DICKSON, William J. (1967), <u>Industrial Relations in Super Sony Management</u> London: Nelson.

DICKSON, William J. (1970), <u>Management and the worker</u>, Hawthorne research works.

DRUCKER, Peter F. (1966), The Effective Executive, N/York: Harper & Row

DUBIN, Robert (1974), Human Relations in Administration with readings 4th Ed Englewood Cliffs Prentice Hall

EJIOGU Aloy (1981), Theories of Job Satisfaction and Job Performance: An overview & Critique, London: Hull University Press.

EJIOGU et al (1995), Readings in organizational behavior in Nigeria, Lagos: Malthouse Press Ltd.

ETZIONI A. (1964), Modern Organizations, N. J.: Prentice Hall Inc. Englewood Cliffs.

FAPOHUNDA. (1996), "Notes on Comparative Management"

FAYOL, Henri (1916), Translated (1949), General Industrial Management, London: Constance Storrs: Sir Isaac Pitman & Sons Ltd.

FEILDER, F. E. (1964), A Contingency Model of Leadership Effectiveness, N. Y. Academic Press Academic Press.

FEILDER, F. E. (1967), Theory of Leadership Effectiveness, N. Y.: McGraw-Hill

FESTINGER, Sigmund Feud Leo (1957), The Theory of cognitive Dissonance, Stanford.

FILLERY, Alan C. (1978), Complete Manager: what works when? Middleton: Green Briar.

GELLERMAN W. S. (1968): "Management by Motivation A. M. A. NY p 286

GEOFREY, G. M. et al (1996), The Practice of Entrepreneurship, Lagos: University of Lagos Press.

GILBRETH, LILLIAN M. (1972), Modern Business Enterprise,

Harmounsworth: Penguin.

HERZBERG, Fred (1966), Work and Nature of Man, Cleveland: World Publishing Company.

HERZBERG, Fred (1968), "One More Time: How do you Motivate Employees" Harvard Business Review

HICKS G. HERBERT & Gullett C. Ray, (1981), Management London: Pitman Ltd. McGraw-Hill Inc.

HOUSE, J. Robert, (1971), "A Path-Goal Theory of Leadership Effectiveness", Administrative Quarterly, PP 321-38.

HUSE, Edgar F. (1979), The modern manager, St. Paul West Publishing Company.

ISHIKAWA, Kaoru (1982), Guide to quality control Asian productivity Organization

JONES, T. O. & Sassier W. E. (Nov - Dec 1995 Ed.) "Why satisfied Customers Defect" Harvard Business Review.

JOSEPH and Susan Berk, (1951): TQM: Implementing Continuous Improvement Sterling Publishing Co. Inc. NY PP7

JOSEPH and Susan Berk, (1991): Managing Effectively, Sterling Publishing Co.

JURAN, Joseph M. (1989), Juran on leadership for quality, N.Y.: Free Press.

KATZ Daniel & Kahn R. L. (1960), The Social Psychology of organizations, N.Y. John Wiley & Sons Inc.

KATZ, ROBERT L. (1970), Management of the Total Enterprise N. J.: Eaglewood Cliffs.

KAZMI, A. (1992), Business Policy, New Delhi: Tata McGraw-Hill Publishing Co. Ltd.

KOONTZ Harold, 1961 (1964), Toward A Unified Theory of Management, N.Y. McGraw-Hill Book Company.

KOONTZ Harold et al (1980), Management 7th Ed, Tokyo: McGraw-Hill books Company Mitchell, 1982.

KOONTZ H. (Dec. 1961): "The management theory jungle", Journal of the Academy of Management vol. 4 No 3, PP 174-188.

KOONTZ H. & H. Weihrich (1988), <u>Management 9th Ed</u>, Singapore: McGraw-Hill.

LAWLER III E. Edward (1973), <u>Motivation in work organizations</u>, Belmont, California: Wadsworth Books.

LAWRENCE Paul & Lorsh J. W. (1969), <u>Developing organization: diagnosis and action reading</u>, Mass.: Addison-Wesley.

LAWRENCE, Paul & Lorsh Jay. W. (1972), <u>Managing group & inter- group relations</u>, Homewood: Richard D. Irwin.

LEAVITT, J. Harold (1972), <u>Managerial Psychology: an introduction to Individual, Pairs, Group in Organization</u> 3rd ed. Chicago University Press.

LEWIN, Kurt (1936), <u>Principle of Topological Psychology</u>, N.Y.: McGraw-Hill

LEWIN, Kurt (1947), <u>Readings in Social Psychology</u>, N.Y.: Rine & Winston.

LIKERT, Rennis (1961), <u>New Patterns of Management</u>, N.Y.: McGraw-Hill.

LUTHAN, F. (1979), <u>Organizational Behavior, 5th edition,</u> N.Y.: McGraw-Hill

LUTHAN, F. (1977), "A General Contingency Theory of Management" <u>Academic of Management Journal</u>, pp. 181-195.

MASLOW, Abraham (1943), "A Theory of Motivation", <u>Psychological Review</u>, Vol. 50.

MASLOW, Abraham (1945), <u>Motivation & Personality,</u> N.Y.: Harper & Row Publishing Company Inc.

McCLELLAND, David (1971), <u>The Dynamics of Power & Affiliation</u>.

McGREGOR, Douglas (1961), <u>The Human Side of Enterprise</u>, N.Y.: McGraw-Hill

MUNSTERBERG, Hugo (1912), <u>Application of Psychology to Industry and Management</u>.

NEWSWEEK, September 7, 1992: "The Cost of Quality".

NNAMDI H.S. et al (1997), Eminent Administrative and Management thinkers, 2nd edition, AMTITOP Books, Lagos

OLIVER, Sheldon, (1939), The philosophy of Management first published in 1923, N.Y. Pitman.

OSAZE, E. B. (1991), Nigerian Corporate Policy & Strategic Management, Lagos: Sharp print Nigeria Ltd.OUCHI, William G. (1981), Discussed Selected Japanese Managerial Practices adapted in the US environment.

OUCHI, William g. (1981): Discussed Selected Japanese Managerial Practices adapted in the US environment.

OUCHI, William G. (1981): Theory Z: How American Business can meet the Japanese Challenge, Reading, Mass.: Addison-Wesley Publishing Co.

ROETHLISBERGER, Fritz & Mayo (193), "Hawthorne Studies".

ROETHLISBERGER, F.J. & N.J. Dickson (1939), Management and the worker Cambridge Mass.: Harvard University Press.

SAYLES, R. Leonard, (1964), Managerial Behavior: Administration in Complex Organizations NY McGraw-Hill.

SCHEIN, Edgar (1970), Organizational Psychology, N. J.: Englewood Cliffs. Prentice Hall Inc.

SEASHORE E. STANLEY et al, (1967): Management by Participation: creating A climate for personal and organizational development.

SELZNICK, Phillips, (1968), Sociology: a text with adapted reading 4th Ed.

SILVERMAN D. (1978), The theory of organizations, London: Heinemann Educational Books Ltd.

SIMEON, Herber & March J. G. (1958), Organizations, NY: John Wiley & Sons Inc.

SLOAM A. D. (1978), The Theory of organizations, London: Heinemann Educational Books Limited.

SOFER C. (1971), <u>Organizations in theory and practice</u>, London: Heinemann Educational Books Limited

STEWARD, Rosemary (1986), <u>Reality of Management</u>, London: Pan Books Ltd.

SUTTLE J. LLOYD et al (1977): <u>Improving Life at Work: behavioral science</u> Approaches to organizational changes.

TANNEMBAUM Robert et al (1961), <u>Leadership and Organization: a Behavioral science approach</u> NY. McGraw-Hill.

TAYLOR F. W. (1911), "The principles of Scientific Management"

URWICK, L. (1957), <u>Pattern of Management</u>, London: Pitman.

URWICK, L. (1974), <u>Elements of administration 2<u>nd</u> Ed.</u>, London: Pitman.

VECTORSTUDY.COM

VROOM, Victor H. (1947), <u>Leadership & Decision Making</u>, University of Pittsburgh Press.

WALTON, Mary (1986): <u>The Deming Management Method</u>, Perigee Books

WEBBER, Max (1947), <u>The Theory of Social & Economic Organization</u>, N.Y.: Oxford University Press.

WOODWARD, Joan (1958), <u>Management and Technology</u>, London: H.M.S.O.

WOODWARD, Joan (1970), <u>Industrial Organization: Behavior & Control</u>, London: O.U.P

ZALEZNIK, Abraham (1966), <u>Human dilemmas of leadership</u>, N.Y.: Harper & Row.

ZALEZNIK A. et al (1973), <u>Distribution of authority in formal organizations</u>,

Aafin International LLC - USA
Aafin Limited - Nigeria

To CLEARLY BUILD THE BEST RELATIONSHIP ON <u>TRUST</u>, BRANCH OUT INTO NEW

NEIGHBORHOODS BY ENGAGING IN INVESTMENTS THAT KNOW NO FRONTIERS.

To BE A WINNER BY DELIVERING MORE REAL VALUE PRODUCTS AND SERVICES

THROUGH OUR HIGHLY MOTIVATED STAFF; USING MODERN TECHNOLOGY.

To SATISFY OUR CUSTOMERS, SATISFY OUR CUSTOMERS AND SATISFY OUR

CUSTOMERS" AROUND THE GLOBAL VILLAGE.

To achieve this:

- ☐ We will run faster and work smarter

- ☐ We will stretch beyond all the known limits

- ☐ We will not prove the paradigms; but create them

- ☐ We will create imaginative thinking in every corner

- ☐ We will engage in brilliance of delivering total quality products and services at moderate charges for moderate returns and for the benefit of HUMANITY.